The Focusing-Oriented Counselling Primer

Campbell Purton

PCCS BOOKS
Ross-on-Wye

First published in 2007

PCCS BOOKS Ltd
2 Cropper Row
Alton Road
Ross-on-Wye
Herefordshire
HR9 5LA
UK
Tel +44 (0)1989 763 900
www.pccs-books.co.uk

The Focusing-Oriented Counselling Primer

A CIP catalogue record for this book is available from the
British Library

ISBN-13 978 1 898059 82 0

Cover design by Old Dog Graphics
Printed by Cromwell Press, Trowbridge UK

CONTENTS

Dedication

To my students on the UEA Counselling and Focusing Diploma courses who have helped me to integrate the thinking with the experiencing.

> If our direct touch with our personally important experiencing becomes too clouded, narrowed or lost, we go to any length to regain it; we go to a friend, to a therapist, or to the desert. For nothing is so debilitating as a confused or distant functioning of experiencing. And the chief malaise of our society is perhaps that it allows so little pause and gives so little specifying response and interpersonal communion to our experiencing. (Eugene Gendlin (1962/1977) *Experiencing and the Creation of Meaning*, pp. 15–16)

INTRODUCTION

COUNSELLING

Before we launch into focusing-oriented ways of working, it might be helpful to take a look at some definitions of counselling itself. It is important to locate the helping activity of counselling in relation to other helping activities in order to avoid confusion regarding the purpose of this book. This book is specifically aimed at people wanting to learn about focusing-oriented counselling with no previous experience or knowledge of counselling or psychology. The key word here is counselling.

So what do we mean by counselling?

What is counselling for?

One way of defining counselling is to look at what it is useful for. In the past thirty years, counselling has become ubiquitous, and it is perilously close to being presented as a panacea for just about everything. Some critics say that the emerging 'profession' of counselling has much to gain for claiming, on behalf of counsellors and therapists, that counselling *is* good for everything. It would be wrong to make such claims: counselling has its limits and part of being a counsellor is to know what those limits are. The problem is that when we are in distress, it is comforting to think that there is a simple answer around the corner.

The situation is not made any easier when we understand that simply sitting down and taking time out from a busy life can make things seem better. Counsellors must be able to explain to their clients the differences between this very important relief and comfort that can be gained from compassionate human contact on the one hand, and counselling as a specialist activity on the other. Counselling can help people in certain states of distress and usually involves change:

 • change in the way the client sees things or themselves

- change in the way a client thinks about things or themselves
- change in the way a client feels about things or themselves
- change in the way a client behaves

Although many people will not be able to put it neatly into a few words, what they seek from counselling can be roughly summarised in a few categories:
- support
- recovery
- problem-solving
- gaining insight or self-awareness
- developing new strategies for living

The sort of distress that counselling can help is often called 'emotional' or 'psychological' and can include:
- stress—a very general and possibly over-used term, but there are some situations in life, especially those that you can't control, that might leave you feeling so stressed that it interferes with your everyday life
- conflict—at home or work
- bereavement—whether a relative or friend. Indeed, having anything permanently taken away might lead to a feeling of bereavement, such as losing your job or losing your ability to do something like walk, play sport or have sex
- depression—another over-used term and not one to be taken lightly. Many life events can make us feel low, and talking it over really does help. The popular term 'depression' can cover everything from feeling understandably low after having your purse stolen or losing your job, through to being unable to get up in the morning or eat properly because you think life is not worth living
- coping with poor health, e.g. having a long-standing health problem or receiving a diagnosis of a serious or terminal illness
- trauma, e.g. surviving (including witnessing) something very disturbing (including abuse of various forms)

What counselling is not for

When someone decides to attend counselling sessions, they are, by definition, distressed. It is, therefore, particularly important that the client doesn't have either their time wasted or their distress increased by attending something that we might reasonably predict would be of no help.

As we have already seen, it is difficult to honestly predict whether counselling will definitely help in a particular circumstance. Nevertheless there are times when counselling is clearly not the first or only appropriate INTERVENTION. It is doubly difficult to appear to turn someone away when they arrive because sometimes:

- part of their distress might be that they have difficulty feeling understood and valued
- they may lack self-confidence and a rejection would damage it even more
- they have been to other types of helper and they think that counselling is their last hope
- they are so desperate they might consider suicide

However difficult it might be, we have to be completely honest with clients if we think counselling is not going to help. It would be wrong to let them find out after a number of sessions, after which they might feel that they are to blame for not trying hard enough. The use of counselling should be questioned if it is likely that their symptoms of distress are caused by:

- poor housing or homelessness
- poverty
- lack of opportunity due to discrimination or oppression

Problems of this nature are best addressed by social action. The counsellor as a citizen shares responsibility with all other members of society to remove these blocks to peoples' physical and psychological well-being.

It would be convenient if we could divide problems up into two neat categories; those of psychological origin (and amenable to counselling) and those of non-psychological origin (and therefore not amenable to counselling). However, there are some other causes of distress which, although they will not be *solved* by counselling, will undoubtedly be helped by counselling in that the person concerned will be able to function better with the kind of support that counselling can provide. It may also be that the client experiences repetitive patterns of self-defeating thoughts and behaviour which renders them less effective in dealing with problems which do not have a psychological origin. It might also be that a person would be better able to challenge an oppressive system if they felt personally empowered, and counselling can sometimes achieve this. Such problems include those caused by:

• poor health (a physical illness or ORGANIC CONDITION)
• oppression and discrimination, including bullying
• living in an abusive relationship

Counsellors must be constantly vigilant to ensure that their work with a particular client or clients in general is not contributing to disadvantage, abuse and oppression by rendering people more acceptant of poor conditions, whether at work or at home.

> Psychologists must join with persons who reject racism, sexism, colonialism and exploitation and must find ways to redistribute social power and to increase social justice. PRIMARY PREVENTION RESEARCH inevitably will make clear the relationship between social pathology and PSYCHOPATHOLOGY and then will work to change social and political structures in the interests of social justice. It is as simple and as difficult as that! (Albee, 1996: 1131, cited in Davies & Burdett, 2004: 279)

What is 'personal growth'?

Counselling in the UK has become associated with what might be called the 'personal growth industry'. Self-improvement has been a feature of our society for a hundred years or more and includes such initiatives as the Workers' Education Association supporting the educational needs of working men and women. More recently further education has embraced more non-vocational courses and reflects the fact that as we get more affluent we have to attend less to the business of mere survival. We can turn our attention to getting more out of life and along with other self-development activities, improving our psychological well-being proves to be a popular choice. Furthermore, when people have a good experience as a client, they sometimes see that learning to be a counsellor could be a further step in self-improvement.

This 'personal growth' use of counselling contrasts with counselling as a treatment for more acute forms of psychological distress as listed on pages 2 and 3 above. It is, however, no less worthy or ultimately useful. Fulfilled, happy citizens, able to put good helping skills back into their communities are an asset, not a handicap.

USING THE GLOSSARY

You may have noticed that some words are set in SMALL CAPITALS. This indicates that the glossary on page 108 carries a brief definition and explanation of the term. The SMALL CAPITALS can appear anywhere in the texts, quotes, subtitles or index.

1

THE ORIGINS OF
FOCUSING-ORIENTED COUNSELLING

Focusing-oriented counselling (F-OC) is a relative newcomer to the world of counselling, at least in the UK. It is deeply imbued with the spirit of the PERSON-CENTRED approach but is not itself a 'school' of therapy or 'brand' of counselling amongst the others. Rather it brings to any kind of therapy a distinctive atmosphere in which the activities of the therapist are always oriented towards the lived EXPERIENCING of the client. It is a way of working with clients that can be incorporated into almost any form of therapy—almost any therapeutic procedure can be carried out in a focusing-oriented way and then that procedure is likely to be more effective than it would be otherwise. Later in this book we will look in more detail at how focusing-oriented counselling relates to the different schools of therapy and if you have an interest in a particular school you may then want to explore further what focusing can bring to that particular way of working.

The origins of F-OC go back to the work of Carl Rogers and his associates at the University of Chicago Counseling Center in the 1950s. Rogers (1957, 1958, 1959, 1961) was concerned with the fundamental question of what made for effective therapy. At the time, the main approaches to therapy were the psychodynamic approaches, behavioural modification, and the new 'non-directive' approach of Rogers himself, which involved close listening to and REFLECTION of what the client said. All the approaches seemed to have some measure of success, but it was not clear what the effective ingredients of therapy actually were.

Rogers and his associates responded to this situation by recording thousands of therapy sessions and studying them in order to see what common elements were present in those sessions that were therapeutically more successful. Out of this work evolved Rogers' best-known conclusion: that what is most important for therapy is not what the client talks about, nor the theoretical orientation of the therapist, but the general attitude and relationship which the therapist has with the client. If the therapist is able to accept the client in a non-judgemental way, to empathise with the client, and to be genuinely present to the client, then the most important conditions for therapeutic change are present. These three conditions later became known as the 'CORE CONDITIONS' of successful therapy. (See e.g. Mearns & Thorne, 1988/2007; Merry, 2004). They are the conditions the *therapist* needs to embody, although Rogers added that there are further conditions that need to obtain on the client's side. (We will come back to 'the client's side' shortly as this is strongly emphasised in F-OC). Rogers and his associates collected much evidence that the *CORE CONDITIONS* really are important in counselling, and this is widely accepted today by therapists of many schools. However, it was not Rogers' claim that these conditions *by themselves* bring about therapeutic change. That, according to Rogers, comes primarily from the 'ACTUALISING TENDENCY' of the client, the inherent tendency of clients to resolve their problems, to 'grow' or 'move forward'. What the CORE CONDITIONS do is help to dissolve the blockages which this ACTUALISING or 'LIFE-FORWARD' TENDENCY runs into.

The discovery of the CORE CONDITIONS was a landmark in the development of counselling, and the conditions are increasingly accepted as a foundation for any helpful therapeutic interaction. On the other hand it seems clear that not *all* clients make progress even when the CORE CONDITIONS are present. There is a great variety in how clients respond to what is offered to them. Rogers himself said that not only must the therapist offer the CORE CONDITIONS but also the client must *perceive* the empathy and acceptance that is being offered to them. Here there is a problem: the more disturbed the client is the less likely they are to be able to perceive the therapist as genuinely accepting and understanding. Yet even where there is no such perception it seems that the interaction with the therapist can be helpful.

From a focusing-oriented point of view the interaction with the therapist makes a difference to the client's EXPERIENCING, however the client *perceives* that interaction. There is also the problem of how much it will the help client if they *do* perceive something of the counsellor's understanding and acceptance yet are unable to 'internalise' those attitudes. If they remain deeply judgemental or ashamed of themselves, then will the therapist's attitudes alone bring about change? In other words, if the CORE CONDITIONS are to 'work' mustn't it be via a process that brings about a change in how clients relate to themselves?

All this draws attention to the importance of the *client's* side of the story. (In their book *How Clients Make Therapy Work*, Bohart and Tallman (1999) demonstrate the importance of this beyond reasonable doubt.) Rogers for many years referred to his approach as 'client-centred therapy', yet curiously so much of the emphasis in this tradition has been on what the *therapist* is or does. One of the things that F-OC does (in relation to the person-centred approach) is to restore the balance through giving more emphasis to the role of the client's EXPERIENCING.

The role of the client's EXPERIENCING is the crucial element that was emphasised by Rogers' close colleague Eugene Gendlin. Gendlin's background was in philosophy and before he met Rogers he was interested especially in the general philosophical question of how our immediate *lived experience* of the world is related to our *concepts*, to our *understanding* of the world. Can we understand our experience in different ways? Can we understand it in any way we like? These are large and rather abstract problems, but when Gendlin heard about Rogers' work at the Chicago Counseling Center he realised that here was a group of people who were working experientially in just that area which interested him philosophically. In the counselling sessions clients were being encouraged to stay with their own felt experience, to find their own ways of formulating it, to create their own meanings. Although he was at the time a PhD student in the philosophy department, Gendlin applied to be trained by Rogers and his associates and was accepted. (In connection with being a philosopher, Gendlin recalls Rogers saying at the interview 'You aren't stupid about people, are you?')

With the background of his interest in people's immediate felt experience and his training as a client-centred therapist, Gendlin turned his attention to the problem of clients who don't make much progress in therapy, even though the therapist seems to be offering or embodying the CORE CONDITIONS. Gendlin and some of his colleagues in Rogers' group continued to record large numbers of sessions, and studied them in order to see whether they could identify which sessions were likely to lead to 'success' and which to 'failure' in therapy. What emerged confirmed Rogers' earlier conclusion that it was not the therapist's theoretical allegiance that mattered or what the client talked about. What seemed to be important, apart from the presence of reasonably high levels of the CORE CONDITIONS, was something about the *way* in which the 'successful' clients talked. This special 'way of talking' provides a good way in to understanding F-OC.

2

A SPECIAL WAY OF TALKING

There is a difference between *what* clients talk about and *how* they talk about it. What they talk about, the *content* of what they say, might involve, for example, childhood memories, their current relationships, their relationship with the counsellor, their worries, their plans, their disappointments and so on. But *what* clients talk about doesn't make much difference to whether they make therapeutic progress. This was one of Rogers' early conclusions, and it has been confirmed by more recent research (Orlinsky et al.,1994).

In addition to the differences in content there can be striking differences in the *way* clients talk. This is something that counsellors often notice early on in their careers. In discussing a client, a trainee counsellor may say, 'He talked a lot about his relationship with his father but it was all very intellectual—I couldn't get much *feel* for the relationship', or 'This morning she again told me the story of her week, and some interesting things had happened, but that's about all she ever does—tell me stories', or 'He has all these plans for self-improvement—he is going on all these courses—it's like he's in training for something, but I can't get any sense of what it's all for', or 'She just came back again to her anger with her partner and his lack of interest in her and their quarrels—round and round—she has expressed these feelings so many times I don't know any more how to respond.'

In situations like these the counsellor may be providing support for the client in their difficulties but at the same time may feel a bit uneasy. Is there anything really therapeutic going on? Perhaps there is, but it also feels that something is missing. The trainee may find themselves saying to their supervisor with some exasperation (and perhaps guilt at being exasperated!), 'I don't feel that this client is really engaging with their difficulties—they are just INTELLECTUALISING or telling stories, keeping busy, wallowing in their emotions.'

The trainee feels that doing these things isn't what counselling is centrally about. But what are clients doing when they are *not* doing any of those things? How does it show up when the client is doing something that *is* recognisably therapeutic? In fact, it is not hard to spot the clients who are engaging more therapeutically, even on a tape of a session and sometimes even on a transcript.

Consider the following four fragments from sessions:

1. Fred said to me, "You really don't need to feel bad about it", but I said I still do, you know, and then he said I shouldn't be so silly. Then Mary chipped in and said, "Still it really would help if someone could at least take her to the hospital on Friday", and that really did make me feel bad and I nearly gave in, but then I thought I could fit it in with going to Sainsbury's, because I really need to get some things in for the children coming at the weekend—they don't come up often, you know, especially now that Anthony is starting that new job in Epping …

This belongs largely in the story-telling mode, though there are some references to her own feelings. What is missing? One suggestion would be that she doesn't 'stay with' her feelings. We will need to look at what that might mean.

2. I think that this guilt I feel is not coming from my own values, so it must be coming from what I've taken in from other people. I think have introjected a lot from my parents, especially from my father, who was always making me feel guilty in a subtle sort of way. But then he was like that because of all that trouble with his brother who died, and my mother was so concerned about him that she didn't give me the attention I needed. So I think I also have an attachment problem …

This belongs in the 'speculating' or 'INTELLECTUALISING' mode. The client is, in a way, giving close attention to what he has experienced. But although he talks about his feelings, analyses them, speculates about them, there is something missing. He doesn't seem 'in touch with' his feelings—he only talks *about* them. Again, we will try to clarify this difference.

3. I'm still just so *angry.* I went to the group again—you know, the one where people are encouraged to let out their feelings. And I knew the anger was still there, so they said, "You need to let it out some *more.*" So I had the tennis racquet and the cushion again and hit it and hit it. I got blisters on my hand—look! But the anger hasn't gone away [raised voice]—I'm still angry—they say you have to get in touch with your feelings but I *am* in touch with my feelings and it doesn't do any good!

This belongs in the 'caught in emotion' mode. In a sense the client is engaged with his feelings, but is it really engagement? He seems more *swamped* by his feelings—as if the feelings are fully there but there is not much *else* of him present.

4. I feel really guilty about not helping out while Fred's in hospital … it's funny … I know I'm not really obliged to and I know Fred wouldn't mind … but I still feel this … guilt … (pause) … well, it's not exactly guilt, I really don't think I'm doing anything wrong … but there's a sort of bad feeling I get … Am I afraid of what they'll say? … No … it's not quite that … No. I really don't care what they'll say … I don't know … I feel all wrong in myself … as if it's wrong for me to decide for myself … you know, just me saying "I'm doing this, so there!" … that feels scary … Yes … I feel scared … it's more fear than guilt … it's me scared of being me.

This is different. If we merely glance at the transcript it *looks* different. There are those ELLIPSES (…) which record where the client has paused and is … is doing what? We will come back to that in the next chapter.

It is this last way of talking which Gendlin and his colleagues picked up as being typical of clients who make more effective therapeutic progress. Through studies of tapes of just the first couple of sessions the investigators could predict with some confidence which clients would make significant progress. Even without the results of these studies I think that most counsellors would sense that what is going on in (4) is more likely to be therapeutically effective than what is going on in (1), (2) or (3). Nevertheless, intuitions of this sort can be wrong, so that it is important that there are the detailed research findings. (More on this in Chapter 12.)

One way of expressing what it is that the more successful clients do would be to say that they make more direct reference to their felt EXPERIENCING. The client who is simply EXTERNALISING talks about the events of their week in an 'external' way gives most of their attention to the narrative of the story and does not give much attention to how they were feeling at the time or to how they are feeling as they tell the story. Similarly, the client who analyses their situation may speak *about* their feelings but does not speak *from* the feelings. The client who simply emotes is different, but they are typically reliving old emotions without connecting to how it all feels right now, freshly, today. In all three cases what seems to be missing is an ability to be in touch with one's immediate felt EXPERIENCING and especially with that EXPERIENCING as a whole. Some people may not know that such a thing is possible—to simply notice 'how things are for me right now', 'how I am in relation to this problem'. And even those of us who do know that it is possible do not always retain this kind of awareness when involved in a difficult situation.

There are degrees of this sort of awareness and one way of investigating it was developed by Gendlin and his colleagues in the early days of what is now called focusing-oriented therapy. For research purposes a scale was developed for measuring a client's 'EXPERIENCING LEVEL' (Klein et al., 1969; Klein et al., 1986). At the low end of the scale the client speaks of external events in a detached way; at the middle of the scale there are more personal reactions and the client is more emotionally involved, while at the high end the client is able to access and integrate all aspects of their EXPERIENCING in a vivid and confident way. This scale, known as the 'EXPERIENCING SCALE', has been used in many studies of the effectiveness of counselling. Like any scale it has its limitations but there can be little doubt that it does 'catch' something of the differences that exist in how clients speak about their problems and especially to what extent the client refers to their own immediate feelings and sensings.

In working with the EXPERIENCING SCALE, Gendlin and his colleagues found that the clients who made best progress tended to be those who had high EXPERIENCING LEVELS (Gendlin & Tomlinson, 1967; Gendlin et al., 1968; Mathieu-Coughlan & Klein, 1984; Klein et al., 1986; Durak et al., 1997). It was not so much that counselling increased client EXPERIENCING LEVEL (although that can sometimes happen) but that those who *began* with a higher EXPERIENCING LEVEL were more likely to do better. This result was disturbing: it meant that for some clients one could be fairly sure in advance that they would be unlikely to benefit much from counselling. However much the counsellor was 'offering the CORE CONDITIONS' the clients were not making use of their interaction with the counsellor in a way that would be likely to help them. The questions then were: (a) what exactly is in involved in the 'higher EXPERIENCING LEVEL' that successful clients seem to have? and (b) can the potentially unsuccessful clients be helped to do what the more successful ones do naturally?

The rest of this book is, in effect, a response to those two questions.

3

THE IDEA OF A 'FELT SENSE'

In this chapter, and the following two chapters, we will be looking at some of the basic concepts of F-OC. If you are new to focusing it may be best to jump now to Chapter 6 in order to get a better sense of what focusing actually is and to try it out a bit, *experientially*. It can be hard to appreciate the importance of the concepts and of the distinctions being made without having had the relevant experiences. On the other hand you may be the sort of person who doesn't want to waste time trying out experiential things that don't (yet) make much sense, in which case it may be best to continue from here! Either way, it may be as well to warn you (or reassure you) that focusing does require close attention to the specific detail of one's EXPERIENCING and, correspondingly, we need to make quite fine distinctions in the concepts we use in thinking about it.

In the previous chapter I referred to the fact that in the more successful therapeutic sessions the client seems to be doing something that many counsellors would describe as 'staying with their feelings' or 'engaging with their feelings'. Of course, other things can also help—we will return to that point in Chapter Five—but the engagement with feelings seems to be centrally important in effective counselling.

Unfortunately, the word 'feeling' in English covers several different kinds of experience and this can be confusing. It will help to sort out some of these different kinds of 'feelings' especially since F-OC is centrally concerned with one particular kind of feeling that is called a 'FELT SENSE'. Such a 'sorting out' of concepts is something that philosophers are especially concerned with, but the philosophical work can have a real impact on clinical or scientific conclusions (Bennett & Hacker, 2003).

One group of feelings comprises *bodily sensations,* for example pains, itches, tingles, giddiness, a sinking feeling in the stomach, felt muscle tensions, jitteriness. These feelings are felt in the body; they are often located in particular parts of the body, although some, such as giddiness or jitteriness may have an 'all-over' bodily quality. Such feelings may result from physiological causes (and they presumably all have a physiological aspect to them) but they may also be characteristic of certain emotional states. For instance, jitteriness could arise from drinking too much coffee, or it could be a manifestation of being *scared*.

This brings us to a second group of feelings—the emotions. We need to distinguish first between emotion manifested in behaviour and *felt emotion* (Gendlin, 1997, pp. 95, 218). Your hope that it will not rain tomorrow may be manifested in your going ahead with the preparations for the outing while also making some alternative arrangements in case it does rain. You might not have any particular *feelings* as you go about these activities. On the other hand, if someone asked you whether you really do feel hopeful about the weather tomorrow, you might pause and consider, 'Am I really hopeful, or am I just going ahead regardless? … hmm … yes … I really do feel quite hopeful.' (Having emotions in *this* way seems to be something characteristically human. A cat notices that a big dog is approaching and prepares to run. It is aware of the dog, and it is afraid, but it is not aware of its fear. It cannot think to itself, as a human being can, 'Ah, there is that fear again. I wish I didn't feel that so strongly.') In what follows we will be concerned with *felt emotion*, not emotion-in-behaviour.

Emotions are characterised by being *about* something or other (Gendlin, 1973; Purton, 2000). When you are afraid you may experience various bodily sensations, such as a tightness in the chest, but that tightness can't be *identified with* the fear. You might get a similar tightness when you are angry, and there may also be occasions when you are afraid of something but you don't have that tightness at all. It is not the particular bodily sensations that make an emotion what it is but *what the feeling is about.* For example, the tight feeling is *fear* if it is a feeling of the situation being dangerous, it is *anger* if it is a feeling that there has been some kind of violation; what makes it *remorse* is the feeling of having done something bad and wanting to make amends; *embarrassment* is the feeling of having done something socially inappropriate. If you are proud of something that you have done you may feel a tingly-bubbly sensation but what makes it *pride* is that a good thing has been done and *you* did it. Emotions in general go with *kinds of human situations*; the emotion-words are names for the feelings of common situations. Less common situations don't have their special words but we can refer to them by longer phrases such as 'the feeling you get when someone gives you a present that you don't want'. That is a distinct emotion but it happens not to have a name in English.

Emotions and bodily sensations are different yet closely connected. It is obvious that some bodily sensations are fairly characteristic of some emotions. Fear often involves sensations of tightness or a sinking sensation in the stomach. Our bodily sensations can tell us something about our emotions (Bennett & Hacker, 2003, p. 215). For example, the lump in your throat tells you that you are going to miss someone more than you realised, or the burning in your cheeks may make you realise that you really are ashamed of what you did. On the other hand it would be hard to say what bodily sensations characterise remorse as distinct from embarrassment, or pride as distinct from joy, or what the bodily sensations of wistfulness characteristically are. It is not the kind of body sensation that makes an emotion *that* emotion. It is *that* emotion because it is a feeling of *that kind* of situation.

It is because emotions are the *feelings* of kinds of situations that we feel differently when our situation changes. Then again, if we can work with our feelings in a way that brings about emotional change our situation will be a different situation. If we come to feel that our domineering boss is actually a very insecure person, so that our emotional response shifts from fear to pity, then our situation is no longer what it was prior to that shift in our feelings.

Much of counselling involves such emotional shifts or changes in the patterns of our feelings. It is then an important question how these shifts come about. In counselling our emotions *change*, but how is this possible? How can fear change to pity? If emotions were simple chunks of feeling this would not be possible, any more than a chunk of lead can turn into a chunk of cheese. The focusing-oriented view is that emotions are best regarded not as 'things' but as aspects of something much more intricate (Gendlin, 1973). Emotions are the feelings of situations and situations are endlessly complex. We might describe a situation as dangerous but that only catches the broad outline of it. For example, the situation *is* dangerous but not so much for me as for other people on whom I depend; then also the danger is not immediate—it is more that something is likely to build up if nothing is done; and then there is another aspect that if it *does* all build up and there is an explosion, in a way it would be a good thing because then those other long-neglected possibilities will be reopened. There is all that intricacy in the situation and there is a corresponding intricacy in the emotion: I feel afraid, not exactly for myself, yet in a way it *is* for myself because I depend on the people who are threatened. It is not an urgent, panicky fear but more of a long-term anxiety, and then there is in it a surprising sense of excitement which, as I give attention to it, I realise is to do with the new possibilities that could be opened up.

The intricacy of the emotion is the intricacy of the situation and any situation is indefinitely intricate. However much we spell out or make EXPLICIT what the situation is there will always be more that could be said. And we can always spell things out in *different* ways—yes, the situation is dangerous, but looking at it another way it is exciting. 'Dangerous' suggests something to be avoided—'exciting' suggests something more positive. These two formulations conflict but the situation, and the feel of it, allow for *both* formulations and for still others.

Suppose I am angry. If I stay with the anger and try to sense what it is about the situation that makes me angry, I may find that the anger is coming out of a deep sense of hurt or that I am to a large extent angry with *myself,* or that the anger is more about a previous incident than about this one. Then if I stay with the hurt or with 'what the anger is really about' new emotions may surface; for example that I am feeling not so much hurt as abandoned, or that what I 'really' feel is resentment. As we go deeper into an emotional response we encounter subtlety or complexity or intricacy of feeling, which soon gets beyond simple labels such as 'angry' or 'sad'. We may then formulate our feelings in new and more intricate ways such as, 'I am feeling the sort of anger that is more at *myself* than at anyone else.' There could be a word for this—perhaps there is in some languages. It would be a word for an emotion more intricate than anger but nevertheless a recognisable emotion.

There is always more to a situation than we can formulate. In focusing terminology we say that there is much in a situation that is *IMPLICIT* rather than *EXPLICIT.* Formulated emotions such as fear, anger, pride and sadness are EXPLICIT, 'just there' and do often seem like 'chunks of feeling'. But in any actual instance of an EXPLICIT emotion there is much that is *IMPLICIT*, and what is IMPLICIT depends on the specific situation and all that is IMPLICIT in *it*. As we stay with an emotion, something of what is IMPLICIT in it begins to emerge.

To put it another way, much of what we know and understand is not in our 'focal awareness', as the philosopher Michael Polanyi (1958, 1967) calls it. It is 'in the background', it is tacit, IMPLICIT, potential. Polanyi—the importance of whose thought has been acknowledged by Gendlin (2001) and Rogers (1968)—has written extensively about the role of the 'tacit' in human knowledge and that notion is crucially important in F-OC. This is because when we have a problem there is much in the problem that is tacit. If we sit with the problem we can draw out different strands, aspects, or facets of it, which are *then* EXPLICIT. Further, which facets we draw out makes a difference to how we see the problem—in fact to what the problem exactly *is* for us. Sometimes the facets that we draw out result in the problem seeming insoluble. And formulated like that, in terms of *those* facets, it may indeed be insoluble. However, this is not the end of the story but can be the beginning. The EXPLICIT version of the problem that we have is insoluble, but there is more to the problem—to any human problem—than has been made EXPLICIT. So what is needed is for us to go back to what is IMPLICIT in the problem and to allow some new formulation of it to emerge. Having tried one formulation unsuccessfully the problem is already a bit different—it is now a problem that has a particular 'solution' ruled out. When we go back to it, it is a slightly different whole.

In focusing, we go one step beyond even the most intricate emotions, or the most intricate formulations of our situation. It is important, but not well known, that there is this 'beyond'. There is *that from which all the formulations arise.* There is the *whole situation* and *the feel of the situation as a whole.* For example, you might start with your feeling of sadness. You ask yourself why you are feeling sad and realise that it is to do with a recent loss. But you sense that there is something more—an image comes from a dream you had last night. It is not obvious how it connects with the sadness. Then it occurs to you how you felt sad *like this* when in childhood you 'did the right thing' and gave away a present to a younger child who wanted it very much. Words from a poem come into your mind, which also somehow connect with the feeling. Here you are experiencing something of the intricacy of that which you initially—and not wrongly—labelled 'sad'. You can sense a whole troubled issue here, which has many facets to it.

Is what you are now experiencing 'an emotion'? Well, there are emotions in it (and also images and sensations and thoughts), but it is a type of feeling that is different from an emotion in that it is not a feeling about a *kind* of situation. As we saw, fear is the feeling of a dangerous kind of situation, pride is the feeling of a having-done-well kind of situation, etc. However, the sort of feeling that we are concerned with here is not a feeling about a *kind* of situation, but about *this* situation. It is the FELT SENSE—to use focusing terminology—of 'all that', of something unique.

Focusing draws attention to the fact that we can feel—or sense—a situation *as a unique whole.* This is not something that happens only in counselling but runs through much of human EXPERIENCING. An example from outside counselling would be: you are in an art gallery and stop in front of a picture that catches your attention. You notice the striking mix of colours and the strong, sharp shapes. You look at the card on the wall, which tells you the name of the artist and the title of the painting. The artist's name surprises you—it doesn't seem to be that artist's style. The title resonates for you in some way that you can't quite place. You notice that the painting has a curious grainy quality and you wonder what technique has been used in the painting of it. Then you stand back and try to take the painting in. All that you have noticed so far becomes IMPLICIT as you try to get a sense of the painting as a whole. You may experience feelings of attraction or distaste for some aspects of it but, if you wait for half a minute or so, a FELT SENSE of the painting may form, a feel of it as a unified whole. There may be no words that quite catch what you now experience but you do *feel* it—*that.* If you then stay with this FELT SENSE words may (or may not) come. Perhaps the word 'wild' comes. That is hardly a description of the painting but it somehow catches the feel of it. Then you feel, 'Hmm … it's not so much "wild" as "unconstrained".' At this point someone comes up to you and asks the way to the toilet and when you return to the painting the FELT SENSE of it has gone. There is just the painting there—the colours and form, the oddity of it being by so-and-so, the curious grainy effect. But you know that you *did* have a FELT SENSE of it and you may be able to get it back. You say to yourself, 'What was it I said it was? … Oh, yes … *unconstrained.*' Now the FELT SENSE comes back—you feel it again.

The general point is that, as well as having emotions, thoughts, sensations, images, etc. in connection with a painting (or a person, or a problem, or a situation, etc.), we can have a FELT SENSE of it as a whole. In a curious way the emotions, thoughts, sensations, images are *in* the FELT SENSE. They are not EXPLICIT but they are *there*, IMPLICITLY.

The FELT SENSE is important in counselling because, in counselling, we are concerned with the client as a whole person and with the client's situation as a whole. To some extent it is possible to work with particular facets of the person or their situation, for example, to work just with their thinking or their emotions or their behaviour, but these facets are *facets of* a whole. For that reason, changes in one facet, such as emotion, will involve changes in other facets, such as thought or behaviour. Many schools of therapy work with one facet or another: what is distinctive about focusing-oriented counselling is that it works also with the *wholes*.

The FELT SENSE is our sense of a problem as a whole. The problem can't be *thought* as a whole because in thinking about it we will draw out only certain facets—and there are endless facets. The only way of 'having it', as a whole, is by getting a FELT SENSE of it.

As we saw in the last chapter, clients who are more successful in therapy tend to pause in their talking. They say things like, 'I felt quite embarrassed … No … it wasn't so much embarrassment as shame … Wow! … this goes quite deep … there's something here I really don't want to look at … [or], Yes, I do want to look at it … but … I need to feel OK enough in myself before I can look at it … but I can't feel OK because … I'm so ashamed … .' In the pauses marked by (…) the client is clearly giving close attention to what they are feeling. They are sensing something there which cannot easily be put into words. The words that do come often *logically* contradict each other (I was embarrassed—I wasn't embarrassed, I don't want to look at it—I do want to look at it), but there is another *non-logical process* going on here. In the pauses between the words the client is dipping into the immediate feel of the situation, into their FELT SENSE of what is there. These places in a counselling or focusing session can be indicated by the ELLIPSIS—the (…) device. Of course not *all* pauses in a session are *that* sort of pause. The client may just be stuck or distracted or daydreaming, or they may be thinking about what would follow logically from what they have just said. Such pauses are of no special interest to us, but the other kind of pause is of great importance. It is the sort of pause in which the client is giving attention to what they are EXPERIENCING. *From the pause* some formulation comes … then they pause again and check … then something else comes … They are 'listening within', attending to something, to their (…), to their FELT SENSE.

As in the case of emotions, the (…) is to some extent felt in the body. In the art gallery you can feel the 'unconstrained' (…) of the picture in your body. There is a *sensation* of being unconstrained in the form of a feeling of release of muscle tension in the chest or in the awareness of taking a deeper breath. In this example, you experience the FELT SENSE *in your chest*. It has a bodily location. On the whole, FELT SENSES are felt in the regions of the body in which we feel our emotions. If you are frightened by a loud noise you probably feel the fear in your chest or stomach not in your ears or elbows. But people are different—pianists may talk of having the feel of a piece of music 'in their fingers'. In his own writings, Gendlin has usually emphasised the central region of the body as the location of the FELT SENSE, but other focusing teachers, such as Ann Weiser Cornell (2005), report that some people experience FELT SENSES in other parts of the body as well, and I also have found this to be so.

It might also be questioned whether the FELT SENSE has to be experienced bodily at all. I think the answer to this is the same as to the parallel question about emotions. There are some emotions in which the BODY SENSE is prominent, especially, for example, intense instances of emotions such as fear or anger. In such cases there may be sensations of being weak at the knees, sick in the stomach, tight in the throat, and so on. With other emotions the bodily sensations are less obvious as, for example, in hoping that it will not rain tomorrow, or being grateful for what someone did long ago (Bennett & Hacker, 2003). Emotions such as these are manifested more in behaviour: your hope that it will not rain is manifested in your making preparations for the outing while also being prepared for rain; your gratitude is shown by the way you keep a person's letters and make a point of sending a Christmas card every year. Yet you *can* turn your attention to how 'all that' feels for you, and you may then sense, for example, a slight bodily excitement in connection with your hope or a slight tearfulness in connection with your gratitude.

The same point applies in the case of FELT SENSES. Sometimes, a FELT SENSE is registered very distinctly in some part of the body— for instance, as 'that sinking feeling I get in my stomach when I think about it all'. In other cases it may be an all-over bodily feeling: 'the whole thing makes me feel squirmy'. Or it may be a feeling expressed as 'There's something wrong with this argument—I can sense it, but I don't know what it is.' A feeling like that may have no specific bodily location—but even then I think that the person does feel a kind of physical unease. There is a spectrum of cases here, but I am inclined to think that the experiencing of an emotion or of a FELT SENSE always brings with it *some* physically sensed difference. Felt emotions and FELT SENSES are *felt*, and feeling does always seem to have a bodily aspect to it.

The references in the focusing literature to the BODY SENSE sometimes causes difficulties for people who hear about focusing for the first time. They may say, 'Yes, I do have a sense of this issue as a whole but I don't sense it in my body—I just have a sense of it.' More research needs to be done on these individual differences and, if after exploring your own responses to situations, you really don't think that you experience FELT SENSES in your body, that doesn't mean you can't focus. You can still give your attention to 'that whole funny feeling I get when I meet him'.

It is sometimes difficult to know whether a bodily sensation is a FELT SENSE or not. The crucial difference is that a FELT SENSE is a sensation that is *of* or *about* or *in connection with* a situation or problem. It is different from a sensation that has been *caused by* a situation. For example, if I have been holding my shoulders in a particular way because of my persistent fear of being criticised at work this may result in tight or painful muscles. Such pain or tightness is a *result* of the situation I'm in, but it is not a FELT SENSE *of* the situation. The FELT SENSE *of* the situation would be a feeling of tightness, probably in the chest or stomach, which comes when I think about my situation. One way of distinguishing a FELT SENSE from other sensations is by imagining that situation to be resolved and asking, '*Now* what do I feel?' If it is a FELT SENSE of the situation, in the imagined change of situation the FELT SENSE will change, but imagination will not remove muscle-tensions *caused* by a situation.

In the next chapter we will begin to look at how all this is relevant in working with counselling clients.

4

FOCUSING: WORKING WITH
THE WHOLE THING

One of the important things that Carl Rogers discovered was that it is often helpful to REFLECT back to a client what they have just said (Rogers 1986a, 1986b). If the counsellor REFLECTS the client's meaning in a rather different form of words the client then knows that they have been understood. The counsellor *must* have understood if they were able to put it like that, in their own words. This helps the client because where we feel understood we feel safe to move on a further step. However, it can also be helpful to the client when the counsellor REFLECTS back *exactly* what the client has said without changing the words at all. In this case the helpful factor is that the client hears their own words back and can then sense whether those words do express exactly what they meant to say.

For instance: a client has been exploring an incident which occurred the day before when he had a conversation with his immediate supervisor at work. He has been over the details of the incident with the counsellor and has said something about his reactions to it. One particular thing that the supervisor said has especially remained with him. He returns to this, giving his attention to the 'feel' of what the supervisor said in the context of the whole situation.

Client:	What strikes me is that, when she said that, I felt a bit *frightened*.
Counsellor:	You felt a bit frightened.
Client:	Hmm ... well, not exactly frightened, but sort of wrong-footed.
Counsellor:	You felt sort of wrong-footed.
Client:	Yes, and kind of ... caught ...
Counsellor:	Kind of caught.
Client:	I can't quite explain it ...
Counsellor:	Mmm ... maybe you can just stay with it.
Client:	I was ... *trapped*.

Counsellor: You felt *trapped*.
Client: Mm … Mmm …
Counsellor: Trapped …
Client: Yes! *Trapped*. That's what was frightening.

There is a recognisable kind of process going on here. We call it a focusing process because the client is focusing on his own EXPERIENCING and also because in the last part something new 'comes into focus'. The client starts with what sounds like a clear statement of what he felt, i.e. frightened. The counsellor REFLECTS this but, when the client hears the words back, it no longer feels that 'frightened' is quite right. It is more like 'wrong-footed' … and also 'kind of caught'. From the simple 'packaged' emotion that he started with—'frightened'—the client has moved into a FELT SENSE of what is there. It is no longer conceptually clear and distinct. He 'can't quite explain it' but clearly it is there—he is referring to *it*. With the counsellor's help he stays with it, 'probes' it, 'taps' it. Then something new comes into focus—it is, after all, a kind of being frightened but the kind that comes from being trapped. Then he can go on to look at how exactly he gets trapped and what is involved in this—it might emerge, for example, that he often feels trapped with certain kinds of people.

When working with a client who responds in this sort of way, all the counsellor needs to do is to REFLECT back what the client says and the client will either say 'Yes, that's it', feel a bit of release and then move on, or he will say 'It's not quite that, it's more like this' and then the counsellor REFLECTS the 'this'; or the client says 'But it's not just that, it's also this' and the counsellor REFLECTS the 'also this'. Each little bit needs saying and when it has been heard and acknowledged the client moves on to the next thing.

This is an important kind of process in counselling. Through it the client moves more deeply into what he is EXPERIENCING, discovers that he doesn't feel quite what he thought he felt or finds new aspects of his EXPERIENCING or of his situation which were not EXPLICITLY there before.

The important aspects of the focusing process seem to be as follows:

SAFETY

The counsellor has created a sufficiently trusting atmosphere or working relationship for the client to feel safe about exploring their feelings. That is, the client can be sure that, as he explores, the counsellor won't jump in with his or her own reactions to the client's situation ('But I don't see what was frightening about it') or criticise ('You shouldn't be frightened of people like that') or speculate ('Of course—she reminded you of your mother') or any of the other things counsellors can do that throw the client off their own experiential track. This first point is the most important one—without it nothing else therapeutic is likely to happen.

'BROWSING'

The client takes some time to talk about his situation. He 'tells his story'. He browses around the situation, noticing various aspects of it, probably having various thoughts about it, perhaps feeling this and that bit of it. This is an exploratory stage prior to focusing itself. But it is a crucial stage—you have to be familiar with something if you are to be able to get a FELT SENSE of it.

GIVING ATTENTION

The client now gives more sustained attention to some aspect of the situation. The situation—like any situation—has many facets to it, but the client is not analysing the situation or getting caught up in the emotions involved. Instead, he is doing something like 'standing back a little from it all' or 'relating to it'. He is relating to his experience almost as the counsellor is relating to him, that is, in a friendly, non-judgemental and non-intrusive way. When it occurs to him that he feels frightened he doesn't say to himself, 'That's silly' or 'That's because she reminds me of my mother.' Instead, he notices the feeling that is there and tries out a particular way of formulating it. He waits, and sees if that way 'resonates' or feels right.

GETTING A FELT SENSE

Then, with the counsellor's help, he stays with the feel of the situation as a whole; he is trying to get a felt sense of it, but the right words don't come easily. He tries 'frightened' and 'wrong-footed' and 'caught' but none of these quite catch it. The initial browsing around is different from what the client is doing now. Now, rather than browsing, he is holding himself ready for something that may come—a little movement, a sense of release, a felt tingling or stirring. As he hears back his words from the counsellor, some of the words elicit such a stirring and the client feels, 'Oh, yes, it really is something like that.' Other words do nothing for him. Then he waits again; a new word comes, he says it, the counsellor reflects it; and then, holding that word there he notices if it brings any fresh movement, any release. This is the heart of the focusing process and we will be looking at it in much more detail later on.

FELT SHIFT

The criterion for whether there has been a forward step is just the sense of release. Sometimes this sense is strongly felt in the body: the client visibly relaxes, or tears come, and the client says 'Oh, so *that's* what it is.' More often, the shift is less obvious, but there may be a deeper breath or a change of expression as the shift occurs. The change often has a physical aspect—the person feels, bodily, a bit different.

The therapeutic process can be thought of as a series of what Rogers (1956, 1961, p. 130) calls 'moments of movement', or what Gendlin (1996, p. 20) calls 'FELT SHIFTS'. These shifts are changes in the client's way of EXPERIENCING the situation. Once a shift has occurred the client may see the situation differently or connect it with other situations in a new way. From the FELT SHIFT may come new insight, but it is the shift in the experience, often registered in a bodily felt change, that comes first. It is not some 'intellectual insight' that leads to things feeling different for the client.

THE BODY SENSE

A FELT SENSE tends to have a bodily aspect to it. It is the 'feel' of the situation sensed at least to some extent in the body. As we saw in the previous chapter, people differ greatly in their degree of awareness of their bodily sensations so that the client may or may not have much awareness of the FELT SENSE in the body. Nevertheless, the FELT SENSE *is* how one is registering the situation and this registering is not something that is done by sight or hearing or any of the specific senses. It is registered in the way that one registers, on walking into a room, that there is someone there whom one really doesn't want to meet. You register, 'Oh, he's there!' not just with your eyes or ears but in your whole body. If you are used to noticing your reactions you may notice a sinking feeling in your stomach but, whether you notice it or not, your body has registered the person's presence. In that way, the FELT SENSE is something physical and focusing is a body process.

RESONATING AND CARRYING-FORWARD

Some things, which the focuser says to themself, or which the counsellor says to the client, result in a FELT SHIFT. Others do not. For example, the counsellor might say, 'It's as if you are stuck in something and can't get out.' The client hears this but it does not *RESONATE* with them. It may in some sense seem true but nothing moves in the client when the counsellor says this. Then the counsellor says, '… or as if you are paralysed …'. and the client sits up and says, 'Yes! *Paralysed*—that's what it is. Paralysed … It's not as if I'm stuck and am trying to get free—I can't even *try* to get free. Something has *happened to me.* As if my engine has been taken out …' The client then goes on to explore the meaning of having had 'his engine taken out' and also—paradoxically— experiences feeling less paralysed. In this episode, the counsellor's second attempt at responding to the client has 'CARRIED FORWARD' the client's EXPERIENCING whereas their first response made no experiential impact.

'CARRYING-FORWARD' is a focusing concept that is closely

related to the notion of what is IMPLICIT. The client was browsing around in his EXPERIENCING and there was something wrong. The wrongness was felt. Saying that he is *stuck* doesn't do anything to the FELT SENSE of wrongness—nothing stirs in response to it. But saying that he is *paralysed* brings a shift. Feeling paralysed was IMPLICIT in what he had been feeling, and the counsellor's words *CARRIED him FORWARD* by allowing the feeling to become EXPLICIT. By contrast, 'feeling stuck' was not IMPLICIT, and so the counsellor's first response did not carry the client forward.

THE UNCONSCIOUS

We only know what was IMPLICIT when it has become EXPLICIT. It is not as if the paralysed feeling was there all along—'lurking in the UNCONSCIOUS'. There was *something* there and the client could feel it, but what was there was precisely a 'something', a (…) rather than a specific, though hidden, feeling of paralysis. This is one of the trickier places in focusing theory but it may give a first indication of how F-OC thinks about what, in PSYCHODYNAMIC theory, would be called 'UNCONSCIOUS feelings'.

In summary, we can say that focusing is the process of getting a FELT SENSE of a problem through giving one's attention to the whole area of the difficulty and then spending some time with the FELT SENSE of it so that new facets of the problem can emerge and CARRY one FORWARD a step. Staying with the FELT SENSE may not result in an immediate resolution of the problem but it can lead to a FELT SHIFT so that the problem is no longer experienced in quite the same way and is therefore no longer quite the same problem.

5

WORKING WITH
THINKING AND EMOTION
IN A FOCUSING–ORIENTED WAY

Focusing involves a new approach to counselling which is not centred on thinking, emotion or behaviour, although all these may have their place at times in F-OC. Rather, it is centred on FELT SENSES and FELT SHIFTS. These are unfamiliar notions to many counsellors and in this chapter I will say a bit more by way of clarifying the ways in which F-OC relates to the more familiar approaches. Some of the issues are discussed further in Chapter 13.

WORKING WITH THINKING

Focusing, as I have explained it so far, is not the only change process in counselling. Another kind of change process involves rational thought. It can be important to identify goals, list possible ways of achieving them, reflect on the thought processes involved in one's attitudes, consider whether they are rational and based on sound evidence. This is the kind of approach that is typical of COGNITIVE-BEHAVIOURAL THERAPY (CBT). F-OC does not deny the value of this approach but draws attention to the reasons why it is often ineffective. The fact is that a person may well work out what the rational course of action would be yet still not *feel* that it is right, or not be able to do what they have concluded is the best thing to do. And that is often the point at which they come to counselling.

The difficulty is that logic and rationality are relative to how our problems are formulated. Once a problem is formulated in a particular way *then* rational thought may be all that is required to reach a solution. For example, *if* the problem is that the client feels trapped in their marriage and wants to leave; if they think it would be best to leave; if they think that leaving will in the long run be best for their partner; if satisfactory arrangements can be made for the children, and so on, then the rational solution is to leave. But there is always far more to a life-problem than can be neatly formulated. The solution may follow logically from the formulation but the formulation leaves too much out. An analogy might be the problem of how many bricks you would need if you were to build a wall. The logic of this is simple: you divide the total volume of the proposed wall by the volume of the bricks. That gives you the number of bricks. But then you build the wall and find that more bricks are needed than you calculated. Something is wrong, but it is not the logic. What has happened is that, as you built the wall, the weight of the bricks made the wall sink into the ground and also to some extent compressed the lower courses of bricks. You formulated the problem in terms of solid ground and incompressible bricks, but that wasn't a good enough formulation. However well thought out our logic may be, the way we picture the problem to ourselves may not sufficiently catch the experiential reality of the situation. And there is *always* more to a situation, and to our EXPERIENCING of it, than can be captured in any formulation of it.

Of course, in a *sensible* rational approach, one keeps this sort of point in mind. At each point in developing the solution one checks back that things are as they were expected to be. If a therapist were working with a client using a rationally constructed DESENSITISATION procedure (see Chapter 13 for an example) it would be sensible to do this regular checking. The client may have formulated their goal clearly and agreed on a way of gradually approaching it, but what if, in the process of this, the client begins to feel that the goal isn't quite what they wanted after all, or that there is something about the means of getting there that now doesn't somehow feel quite right? To continue with the rational plan, regardless of these changes in the client's EXPERIENCING, is clearly *not* sensible. But that means that in any rational or COGNITIVE THERAPY there needs to be a constant checking with the client's FELT SENSE of what is going on. COGNITIVE-BEHAVIOURAL THERAPY can be done in a focusing-oriented way—and to be effective it *needs* to be done in that way.

In *thinking* about our problems, a common mistake is to

proceed from one thought to another in a logical way but never to stop and check whether that step (or where we have got to) feels right from the perspective of the whole. If, instead of moving on to the next thought, we pause and ask, 'And how is all that now?' we may be able to get to a deeper level from which new thoughts may indeed come. But these new thoughts do not follow by logic from the earlier ones; they come from our sense of the whole situation (as changed, no doubt, by our earlier thinking). The new thoughts may *logically* contradict the earlier thoughts, but they are an experiential consequence of what we thought before, after that has been put into interaction with all the rest of our experience.

Suppose we have what seems an insoluble problem. We say, 'I could do that, but … or I could do this, yet … or what about … but no, that is no good … .' We bump against the problem like a fly bumping into the window, but after a period of this painful bumping something new can happen. Instead of formulating *another* possible solution we can stay with the whole sense of all those failed solutions (which in a way define the problem) and allow a sense of *all that* difficulty to come to us. Through thinking intensively about the problem we have an increased sense of it— we can feel the heavy or tangled difficulty of it. There is a sense *of the whole thing* that includes all those aspects that make it a problem, all the reasons why the obvious solutions won't work, all our experience of dealing with related problems, all our knowledge and thinking and reading that is relevant to the problem. That is all there, much of it IMPLICIT rather than EXPLICIT.

The problem, as we originally formulated it, is insoluble. But a formulation of a problem is not the same as the problem itself. The problem itself is a blocking in our *life*, not simply in our thinking. Our formulation of the problem has arisen out of our life, our whole experience, and we can go back into our felt experience, into our life-sense of the problem. Then something new can come. There is never just one way of formulating, conceptualising, thinking about a situation. There can be many ways, although it may be very hard to find one that can carry us forward. If we let go of our current formulation of the problem and dip back into the FELT SENSE of the whole situation there is no guarantee that we will come up with a new formulation that will carry us forward. Yet there is that *possibility* and, if our current formulation of the problem renders it insoluble, the only possible way forward is to let go of that formulation and go down to the place from which formulations come—to our lived experience of the situation.

So the focusing-oriented approach does not disparage thinking. Rather it leads to a kind of thinking that is 'more than logical', a kind of thinking that uses logic but then dips back into the EXPERIENCING from which the logical formulations come.

WORKING WITH EMOTION

A second general kind of approach to counselling centres on the idea of 'following your feelings', expressing emotion, getting in touch with blocked emotion from traumatic childhood events. F-OC accepts the value of all this but questions whether effective therapy is simply a matter of uncovering the past feelings and releasing them. Suppose that, in a particular case, certain emotions from the past have been released. If the client goes back again to those memories the emotion will come again. But what now? For there to be therapeutic movement the relived past has to make a difference in the *present*. The client needs to bring their attention to how it all feels now that the block has been released. The old emotions have come through but it is not very helpful for the client simply to have their current experiences plus the past emotion. What is needed is for the past emotion to be present in a new way in interaction with all that has happened since. The past needs to inform the present in the way that *ordinary* past experiences do. This is what is meant by the integration of the past emotions, but such integration can only happen on a FELT-SENSE level. The client needs to get a sense of how things are for them now that the block has been released. The release is the beginning rather than the end of the process. Of course, counsellors who work with CATHARSIS in a sensible way are well aware of all this, but what they are aware of is just that which F-OC emphasises: the centrality of the whole person and of the whole situation rather than the centrality of emotional release.

It is easy for a FELT SENSE to slide into an emotion. You are thinking about the day ahead, the things you need to do, the people you will be seeing. If you let yourself sense for it you may be able to get an overall sense of how the day feels—'well, sort of OK but a little bit trembly, not so bad taking it all as a whole'. Then the trembliness builds up and real anxiety comes. Now you are experiencing something like an emotion. You are caught in the anxious feeling. This is very different from where you were a minute ago when you were getting a FELT SENSE of your day. In having the FELT SENSE there is a kind of space between you and your emotions. Your FELT SENSE of the day ahead involves emotion, and particularly some anxiety, but in having a FELT SENSE of it you are not exactly *being* anxious; rather you are noticing that there is some anxiety there, along with much else.

There is a big difference between 'emoting', i.e. being caught up in an emotion, and being aware of an emotion. We could say that in being aware of the emotion we are 'detaching' ourselves from it, but that doesn't quite catch what is involved. If we are with another person who is experiencing an intense emotion, we are indeed 'outside' their emotion—it is not *our* emotion. But we need not be observing in a coldly detached way. We may be deeply involved with, deeply connected with, the person. The point is that, while they are 'lost' in the emotion, we can sense the emotion in its context of that person's life and their relationship to us. For them, their EXPERIENCING has narrowed to the having of the emotion whereas for us the emotion is felt in its whole context. Similarly, when we are caught in an emotion ourselves we may be able, not exactly to detach from the emotion, but to regain a sense of the emotion as just one element in the whole of our felt EXPERIENCING.

The point is not to detach from the emotion but to relate to it. Nevertheless, such relating does require a kind of space in which to relate. You have to be able to feel the emotion in relation to the rest of your feelings, your thoughts, your hopes, your beliefs. These form a vast web, or network, of connections in which the emotion has its place. In this space the emotion need not dominate the scene—it can be experienced, but in its place. The feel of it is then, 'Oh, yes, there is my anxiety which is quite strong today and sort of interferes with my relief at that other thing being called off. There also is a bit of annoyance at this anxious thing being there again when I thought I had dealt with it through that session on Tuesday. Hmm … there must be more to it than I thought … Interesting … .'

There is the sense of your situation *as a whole* within which the emotions come. The 'whole' is all the rest of your EXPERIENCING in connection with that situation, all of those interconnected aspects or parts of it. That 'whole EXPERIENCING' is 'you' in a way that the emotion is not. The emotion is just one element or aspect of you. 'Getting a distance from the emotion' is a matter of experiencing it from the perspective of your *whole* EXPERIENCING.

Just as we can go from one thought to another without dipping down into our felt EXPERIENCING, so we can go from one emotion to another in a way that is not helpful. There is a place in therapy for the release of emotion but then the emotion that has come needs to interact with all the rest of our EXPERIENCING. Instead of sensing how we now feel as a whole about the situation, we may simply allow the emotion to repeat or move into another emotion. Having experienced the release of venting our anger we may vent it again and again. Or having become really angry we may now feel scared of what we might do or become depressed. In this sort of pattern it could be said that we are very much in touch with our feelings, yet that is not really true. There is a lot of emoting but very little of the person who *has* the emotions. It is important for the emotions to 'come out', and their coming out will change the situation, but there is no guarantee that the new situation will be better than the old one. The problem may now be worse. More rounds of emotion may lead not to resolution but to increasing chaos.

In emotional states our EXPERIENCING is narrowed (Gendlin, 1973). Emotion focuses our attention in a way that can shift things that would not otherwise shift but the rest of our experience is neglected. Hence, emotional expression can be the *beginning* of the solution of a life-difficulty—it can get us to the point where 'the cards are on the table' and the situation is changed. But now, rather than moving into further emotion, what is needed is to dip down into our wider EXPERIENCING and get a sense of how—overall—things are now different and what might now be a way forward.

In summary, the resolution of personal problems can require hard thinking, LOGIC, rationality; it can also involve emotional expression and CATHARSIS. But neither of these is the whole story. Rather, thinking and emoting can bring us to the edge of the place from which further therapeutic progress can be made. That place lies 'deeper' than both thinking and emoting, it is the place of our lived EXPERIENCING before it becomes formulated in thoughts or manifested in specific emotions. It is the place to which we need to go when neither thought nor emotional expression, nor any combination of these two, can carry us forward.

In the next chapter we will look at focusing as a way of getting to that place. We will begin with the focusing process as it can be practised by oneself. Then in the following chapter we will introduce the idea of a focusing companion—someone who helps and supports you while you focus. Finally, in Chapter 8, we will look at how what goes on in a focusing partnership can be incorporated into counselling sessions.

6

THE FOCUSING PROCESS

Focusing-oriented counselling is counselling that is oriented towards focusing. That is, while many different kinds of things may go on in a F-OC session, there is a background orientation towards helping the client to be in touch with their own EXPERIENCING and to formulate their EXPERIENCING in ways that will CARRY them FORWARD. We will consider shortly the kinds of help that the therapist can provide but first it will be useful to look more closely at the focusing process itself.

This process can, to some extent, be isolated from whatever else goes in the session. It is possible to learn to focus without necessarily being engaged in counselling. One of the earliest accounts of focusing can be found in Gendlin's book *Focusing* (1978/2003), which is not a book about counselling but about how a person can learn to focus and to use focusing in working with their personal difficulties. It is essentially a self-help book rather than a book for counsellors.

Nevertheless, learning to focus can be of great value to a counsellor. In learning focusing we are learning how we can stay with our immediate EXPERIENCING in a way that allows our EXPERIENCING to reformulate itself in a constructive way. It gives us insight into what often goes on for clients when they are making progress in therapy and it helps to familiarise ourselves with the kinds of difficulties that can interfere with the process. What we learn in focusing we may be able to carry over into our work with clients. That will not usually be a matter of teaching focusing to clients but of bringing into our client work little bits of the experience and expertise that we have found to be helpful in working with ourselves and with our focusing partners.

In learning focusing you learn ways in which you might work with yourself; then, when with a client, you *may* find that something in those ways can be helpful to the client. We will look at the details of this later on but first we need to put the focusing process itself under a magnifying glass and look at its various aspects.

What follows is a quick summary of what is involved in learning focusing. If you have never focused before you might want to try it following these guidelines but to learn properly it would be better to follow the more detailed instructions in Gendlin (1978/2003) or Cornell (1996). Most people find it easiest to learn focusing in a workshop context or through having some sessions with a focusing teacher, but it is perfectly possible to learn it from a book. Gendlin's *Focusing* book has sold nearly half a million copies and he still gets notes of thanks from people who say it has saved their lives (Hendricks, 2003, p. 69).

The main purpose of this section is not to teach focusing, but to show the different elements of the process. However, focusing is one of those things that doesn't make much sense without having had something of the actual experience. So I would encourage you to experiment.

CLEARING A SPACE

First, find a quiet place where you will not be disturbed, sit down and relax a little.

It may be helpful to begin with a procedure called 'Clearing a Space'. You won't always need to do this when you focus, but it can bring you to a place from which it is easier to begin focusing. It is also a valuable stress-reduction procedure in its own right.

Bring your attention into your body—notice how you can feel your body being supported by the chair and the floor. Notice your breathing, the rise and fall of your chest. Notice any obvious sensations in your body, such as a tightness in your shoulders or a soreness in your throat.

Now ask yourself, 'How am I feeling right now? How are things for me?', and see if you can sense how you—how your body—responds to these questions. Try the question, 'Am I feeling fine in my life? Am I really comfortable with how things are for me?' Probably you will sense that the answer to this is 'No' or 'Not entirely'. Notice that there is a sense in which your body 'talks back' when you try out these questions. You ask, 'Am I just fine today?' and something in you 'says' 'Well, not really!'

Notice what feels 'not fine'—there is something there, a problem, an issue, a difficulty that stands between you and feeling completely fine. It might be a big and agonising life issue or it might be a problem left over from a disagreement yesterday, or just an irritating niggle about what someone said this morning. Just note this issue. Don't go into it, don't begin to think about it, don't get emotionally caught up in it. Instead just say, 'Oh yes, there's all that thing … that's there.' See if you can set it aside for a while. Some people find it helps to picture the difficulty as a big bundle of stuff (our problems usually have all sorts of things bound up in them). Set this bundle down somewhere nearby. (I remember that as a child we sang in a hymn, 'Bringing all my burdens, sorrow, sin and care/At Thy feet I lay them, and I leave them there.' It is a bit like that.) If the 'burden' is something very painful and sensitive, you may want to cradle it gently rather than setting it down. See what helps. The point is to get a little separation from the trouble so that you can—later on—relate to it.

See if you sense a little release from having set the trouble down. Does your body feel a little bit easier? Can you breathe a bit more freely? If not, then gently try again to set the trouble down.

Then say to yourself, 'Now, apart from *that* difficulty, is everything in my life just fine?' Probably not. Allow yourself to sense what else is standing between you and feeling fine. See if you can set that difficulty down as you did with the first one. Allow yourself to feel any relief that comes … you are taking a holiday from your troubles.

Continue until there seems to be nothing else that stands between you and feeling fine. Sometimes, in addition to particular problems there is a background feeling that is always around—for instance a feeling of always being a bit anxious or a bit sad. If there is something like that, set it out as well.

What you have been doing here is clearing a space for yourself amidst your problems. The problems are still there of course, but you are standing back from them a little, they are not swamping you. You can, as it were, take a look at them without getting caught up in them.

GETTING A FELT SENSE

Now cast your mind over the problems that are sitting there. See if you can sense which one might especially need your attention today. See if the others can wait. You may need to say to yourself that you will—later—give *them* some attention too. But, for now, it is this one that you need to work with.

Bring your attention to *that* issue or trouble. Don't think about it or get caught up in it. Instead, just sense it as a whole—'all that business about so-and-so'. Say to yourself 'That's there … all that thing.' Let yourself feel it as an emotional whole: there will be many facets to it but they somehow belong together on a feeling level and constitute *that* problem. Don't try to analyse the problem but just get a feel of it. It may help to ask, 'What *is* the feel of all this? Does it make me feel constricted, or jittery, or heavy … ? See if you can get some sense of how it feels, of how it is registering in your body. It can often be felt *there,* in the chest or stomach for example. There may be no one word that quite fits the feel of it, but sometimes a combination of words *will* catch that feel—for instance 'tight–closed' or 'shivery–bubbly'. Or maybe no words spontaneously come. Nevertheless, you can notice that the trouble does have a distinctive feel to it. This 'feel' is the FELT SENSE of the trouble. It will probably not be there when you first give your attention to 'all that thing'. But, as you direct your attention to 'all that' and try out words for it, the FELT SENSE forms. The FELT SENSE is not like a feeling of anger, or sadness, which is just there, waiting, when you bring your attention to your EXPERIENCING. Rather it *forms* through your giving your attention to 'all that'. (It is much the same as when looking at paintings. You don't necessarily look at the particular colours or shapes or people depicted, but may rather sit in front of the painting and get an overall 'feel' for it. This painting 'feels different' from the one over there … this one is sort of 'wild and free' while that one is 'precise and contained'. The FELT SENSES of the pictures take a little time to form, but once they have formed they are 'there' as distinctly as an emotion such as anger.)

HANDLE WORDS

The words that catch the feel of the trouble are what Gendlin calls 'HANDLE WORDS': they allow you to get a grip on the FELT SENSE of the trouble. It is easy to lose hold of a FELT SENSE. It *was* there, but now it has gone. A HANDLE WORD can help to bring it back: you say to yourself, 'What was the feel of that … ? Oh, yes, it was "shivery" … can I feel that "shivery" again? Yes, there it is—*shivery*.'

ASKING

Up to here in the focusing process you have been giving your attention to your EXPERIENCING and allowing a FELT SENSE to form. You can't *make* a FELT SENSE form—it has to *come* the way tears come. The active part up to here consists in creating conditions in which a FELT SENSE can come. But now that a FELT SENSE is there you can begin to interact with it. You can gently try out a range of questions and see what response they elicit from the FELT SENSE. Examples of such questions are:

What is it about this problem that makes it so *jittery* (or whatever the HANDLE WORD IS)?

Or, if you have no HANDLE WORD, you can ask,

'What is it about the problem that makes it feel like *this*?'

You direct the question to the FELT SENSE and *wait* for a little bit. Notice if anything stirs in the FELT SENSE. Does it respond at all to this question? Does that question mean anything to the FELT SENSE? See if something comes—a word, an image, a memory, a feeling … welcome whatever comes, don't query it, however odd or inappropriate or irrelevant it might seem. You can *think* about it later. For now just let come what comes.

If the FELT SENSE doesn't respond to that question you can try slightly different questions, such as:

'What really is the crux of this problem that makes it so *jittery*?' (for example).

'What is the worst of this trouble?'

See if something stirs in response to these questions.

If not, you can try a different kind of question. What needs to come may not be what this *is* but what it *needs*. So try questions such as:

'This thing that feels so jittery—what does it need?'

'What might be a step forward from this jittery place?'

'What might help with this?'

You ask these questions in a gentle, patient, friendly sort of way, inviting an answer but not demanding it.

Sometimes nothing will come. It can't be made to come. But, even if nothing comes, you have interacted with the FELT SENSE. Such interaction may bring changes even though nothing seems to have changed right now.

FELT SHIFTS

However, often something does come. Often it is a surprise and sometimes it makes little logical sense. Here is an example:

The focuser starts with a sense of *something uneasy* in their relationship with X.

They stay with it and try to get a fuller sense of it. They let anything come from it that can come.

This is an activity—a peculiar sort of activity. It is not doing anything externally but nor is it analysing, thinking, emoting. It is an activity like 'waiting on' or 'being available'.

Then an image from a dream pops up—a dream in which in which the focuser was angry with X. That has a particular sort of feel to it—an atmosphere. But it goes again. The 'uneasy' feeling is still there, but the dream brought it into focus a bit. (SHIFT 1) The focuser thinks, 'There is something here about how I relate to X—and it is a bit the same with Y … something … It is like … the opposite of 'just doing it'. (SHIFT 2)

That is what has come. It is an odd thought. The focuser is puzzled by it, unsure what it amounts to.

'Just doing it' … just doing what? … But that goes nowhere … Nothing stirs when the focuser asks that question. So they immediately drop it and come back to 'like the opposite of *just doing it*'. The focuser senses that it is the 'just' bit that catches what is crucial … (SHIFT 3)

Ah … yes … With X and with Y what happens is that I get to be … 'not-just'. (SHIFT 4)

There is a wanting to get away from this 'not-just'—that seems related to the anger with X in the dream. (SHIFT 5)

They wait for a while …

There is a longing for 'just'. (SHIFT 6)

'Just'.

What does 'just' mean?—Fair, right … but it's not that sort of 'just' … Another dead end …

It is the 'just' in '*Just* do it', or 'I've *just* arrived', or 'It's *just* right'.

Now they can feel this *just* there, more strongly. (SHIFT 7)

'I need to be in this *just* way—it's like being fresh—"just picked", being in the moment—"just now" … .'

With X and Y something happens—I lose the 'just'. (SHIFT 7)

Something else comes in—what is that?

Ah, that is the uneasy thing. (SHIFT 8)

It's like it sits on the 'just', paralyses it.

That is the problem. (SHIFT 9)

Here the focuser ends with the problem. In a way, the problem is the solution—what was just an uneasiness has become something much more EXPLICIT: there is an important thing in their life called 'just' and something is interfering with that 'just'. Something has changed in their inner space but not (yet) in the ordinary space of everyday life. From outside it may look as if nothing has changed at all. But *everything* (in respect of this difficulty) has changed. From here the focuser can begin to do something in the outside world. For example, they might now remember to hold on to the 'just' feeling when with X or with Y. New possibilities form as this FELT SENSE of 'not losing the *just*' begins to penetrate or infuse the external situation. Or, rather than taking such 'ACTION STEPS' they might go on to another *focusing* step—what exactly is it that paralyses the 'just'? They might stay with that.

The FELT SHIFTS are what Rogers (1956, 1961, p. 130) called 'moments of movement'. They are the stuff of which therapeutic change is made. After such a shift the client's EXPERIENCING is a bit different, *they* are a bit different. When they finish focusing and go out into the world they will be a bit different and *behave* a bit differently, and this will bring new responses from others.

What happens in the focusing session is not determined by any theory, but various theories could be applied to it. Someone who likes Rogers' concepts might suggest the 'just' feeling is a manifestation of the ORGANISMIC VALUING PROCESS and that the 'not-just' is rooted in conditions of worth. Someone who likes PSYCHODYNAMIC notions might understand the shifts in terms of an increasing EGO STRENGTH. A Jungian might see the client as drawing on the ARCHETYPE of the *PUER AETERNUS* which is characterised by spontaneity and freedom from responsibility. These are ways of *thinking* about the process, and each of them could be illuminating, but what brings about the shifts can't be identified with any of these. What brings about the changes is that to which all these, in their different ways, point. It is that which the focuser feels and works with. *That (...).*

WELCOMING AND ENDING

When something comes it is important to welcome it, to receive it in a friendly way, even if it seems wrong, or irrelevant, or stupid. The attitude to what comes needs to be the attitude that a counsellor has to their client—understanding, accepting, open. Gendlin writes in this connection of 'the CLIENT'S CLIENT'. The client—or focuser—needs to be with their FELT SENSE, and what comes from it, in the way a good counsellor is with their client. The FELT SENSE can indeed be thought of as the CLIENT'S CLIENT.

Then, at the end of the session, it may be important for the focuser to 'mark' where they have got to, to say to themselves, 'I can come back to this next time.' Some focusers *thank* what has come at the end, as well as saying *hello* to anything that comes in the session. You may want to experiment with whether these things feel right for you. The only fundamental 'rule' of focusing is not to follow any of the 'rules' rigidly. If any part of the focusing procedure doesn't feel right to do, then try to get a sense of what *does* feel right and do that instead.

DIFFICULTIES IN FOCUSING

Some people find that focusing comes naturally to them, others do not. No 'helpful procedure' works for everyone and if, after experimenting with it, focusing doesn't feel right for you then *of course* it is best to leave it alone. (But that 'of course' itself embodies the focusing principle of listening to one's *own* EXPERIENCING!)

Some of the reasons which I have come across for people 'not liking' focusing are:

- The fear that *awful things* will emerge, that it is better 'to let sleeping dogs lie'. This is an issue in connection with counselling generally and needs to be taken seriously. However, the focusing process is especially well-adapted to situations in which there are such fears. The fear itself is part of the person's situation and is accepted as such, and if deeply disturbing emotions begin to surface the basic focusing procedure involves the maintenance of a comfortable distance from them.

- The feeling that 'I do this focusing thing anyway—it is really precious to me and I don't want to have it taken over or regarded as a technique to be learned.' If you do focusing anyway, then that is fine! But you may still find it interesting to look at the different ways in which people do focusing, and at the issues involved in bringing focusing into counselling. On the other hand you may be doing something, such as 'being aware of your sensations' or 'sitting with your feelings', which is only *rather like* focusing. It could be helpful to compare focusing in more detail with what you do—you can then keep your own thing, and have focusing as well.

- You may not have much awareness of your bodily reactions to situations. As we saw in Chapter 3, this is quite common and there are probably various reasons for it, ranging from early physical trauma or parental discouragement of interest in feelings to a scientific or medical training that emphasises the idea of the body as a machine. If focusing talk of 'feelings in the body' puts you off, then leave aside 'the body' and just stay with 'the feelings'. You can feel angry even if you can't make much sense of the question, 'Where do you feel that anger?'

- You may feel that focusing is too introspective, that it takes you away from your relationships with other people. (Joan Klagsbrun (n.d., p. 1), an American psychologist, has said that focusing is 'GESTALT THERAPY for introverts'!) Certainly there is an inner-directed aspect to focusing but, as we have seen, what we focus on is not so much an inner sensation but the FELT SENSE of our *situation.* In focusing, we are often *staying with how we are in relation to* other people and as we do this our relationship with them actually changes. In focusing theory, the distinction between 'inner' and 'outer' is no longer a simple one.

- People with a rather 'purist' client-centred background may feel uneasy about focusing because it seems 'directive'. In a sense it *is* directive, but it directs the client's attention to their own EXPERIENCING, and that is surely 'client-centred'. The issues surrounding 'directivity' in client-centred or PERSON-CENTRED COUNSELLING are quite complex (Lietaer, 1998, pp. 62–64; Mearns & Thorne, 2000, pp. 190–195; Purton, 2004, pp. 42–45)—one can't just say, baldly, that focusing 'is directive' or that being directive 'is not person-centred'.

This chapter has aimed to give you some feel for the sort of thing that goes on in focusing. Now we will look at how the focuser can be helped and supported by the presence of another person.

7

FOCUSING PARTNERSHIPS

It is quite possible to focus on one's own, and some people prefer to work in this way. But, for many people, it is much easier to focus if one has a companion.

There are good theoretical reasons for this but, on a more common-sense level, we know that the mere presence of another person often does make a large difference to the *quality* of our EXPERIENCING. Depending on the context, their presence may either facilitate our EXPERIENCING or it may shut it down. Think of going to see a film. The film is just beginning but no-one else is there. You feel a bit uneasy and can't quite settle into your experience of the film. Then another person arrives. They smile at you and sit down a few seats away. You do not speak to them but they are there. You have a companion. Now you can relax in your EXPERIENCING of the film. By contrast, imagine that you are standing at the top of a cliff on a summer evening looking out over the sea. You sense the wide expanse of the sky and feel open, free. You feel that the sky and the sea and the light on the water somehow speak to you and draw you into a deeper EXPERIENCING. Then you notice someone a little way off *who is watching you* through binoculars. Now your EXPERIENCING changes completely—it becomes more guarded and closed, it is no longer carried forward by the sky and sea.

When we try to focus, it can help to know that someone else is there with us as a friendly presence. They need not say anything but, if they do, it needs to be a special kind of response—a response that will encourage us to go a step further, or a level deeper. It needs to be a friendly, supportive, interested response that does not add or take away anything. A companion who can be there in such a way makes focusing easier. By contrast, if we have someone with us who makes judgements about our EXPERIENCING, theorises about it, or brings in their own point of view, then our EXPERIENCING is less likely to unfold and deepen. The presence of the other person shuts us down rather than encouraging us to open up and CARRY FORWARD.

Even when we do focus alone, the interpersonal dimension is not entirely absent. Rather than another person responding and helping to CARRY FORWARD our EXPERIENCING, we respond to our *own* EXPERIENCING. We can respond to ourselves because we have been responded to by other people. Human EXPERIENCING *begins* with the mother responding to the infant and *later* the infant learns to respond to itself. Responding to oneself is a subsequent, more sophisticated, development (Mead, 1934; Gendlin 1997). We can do it, and it is part of our humanity that we are able to do it, but the roots of this ability lie in a particular kind of friendly, reflective, supportive interaction with others. Focusing partners try to provide just this kind of interaction.

What the focusing companion primarily needs to do is to listen and to reflect what the focuser has said. Such REFLECTION has two functions. First, it maintains the connection between the focuser and their companion so that the focuser knows that they are not alone with their difficulty. What is being done is something shared, interpersonal. Secondly, the REFLECTION helps the focuser to give attention to their EXPERIENCING and to formulate it in a way that allows it to unfold and CARRY FORWARD. When the focuser hears back what the companion says, one possibility is that they feel, 'Yes, *that's* what it is.' There is a sense of relief—that it has been said and has been understood. It no longer needs to be said, because it *has been* said. The saying of what needed to be said creates a bit of space. Now the next thing can come. But more often, when the focuser hears back what the companion says, they feel 'Well, it's not exactly that … it's more …' or 'Well, it *is* that, but there is another aspect as well …'. These responses may come even if the companion has said back the exact words that the focuser has used. The words seemed to express the focuser's meaning when they themselves said them but now it is a bit different.

If the focuser is very much in touch with their EXPERIENCING it is best to reflect back each thing they say and not to change their words at all. These words have come from *that* exact experience and the focuser needs to hear them back exactly. But often the focuser is trying to get more in touch with their EXPERIENCING. They are browsing around in their feelings, telling little bits of stories, memories, concerns, dreams, and so on. Here the companion needs to reflect the personal meanings, the 'edges', the poignant aspects. In this way the companion helps the focuser to get nearer to what is most important to them right now, in their immediate lived EXPERIENCING. This is the place where focusing can begin. The initial 'browsing' phase is valuable in itself; it has the same sort of function as the 'clearing a space' discussed in the previous chapter. As the focuser browses around in their feelings it tends to become clearer what the most important concerns are.

The next phase begins where the focuser feels that they are in touch with a particular concern with which they would like to work. Any human concern or difficulty will have 'in' it a multiplicity of aspects or facets. There may be an immediate EXPLICIT problem, formulated as, for example, 'I want to leave my job but I can't', but *in* that problem there are all the factors that make him want to leave and all the difficulties with leaving. And in each of those factors there is a further multiplicity—he wants to leave because he doesn't feel appreciated and doesn't get on well with his boss, and anyway this isn't really the sort of work he wants to be doing for the rest of his life, and … . Then within each of *those* there may be a myriad of facets. That feeling of not being appreciated is there in *other* aspects of his life; there is something about him not appreciating *himself*; there is something about this being an *old* feeling; there is some odd thing about whether he really appreciates other people, or, if he *does,* that somehow they don't give back as much as he gives, or … . To make all this EXPLICIT, to formulate it all COGNITIVELY, would take a very long time. More realistically, it simply could not be done, for each facet that comes to light contains *new* facets. Further, the facets are not independent of one another—they are all interconnected in complex and subtle ways. (Here we see one reason why a purely COGNITIVE approach to counselling can't possibly be adequate.)

Yet, in spite of this, *there is* the *problem as a whole.* The focuser cannot grasp it INTELLECTUALLY but they can *feel* it. There is that whole stuck thing that they sense when they think about leaving their job. It feels stuck, heavy. Many people faced with a problem like this do not give their attention to the feel of the problem. They may not realise that such a thing is possible or they may not see any point in doing so. They think, 'What is the point of staying with that vague, stuck, heavy feeling? What is needed is to specify my possible choices, see what the consequences of each choice would be and then act decisively.' But, sadly, this is what they are unable to do. They can't do it because 'something' stops them.

Focusing works with the 'something'. Not (just) with the thoughts and emotions and ideas and sensations that are there but with the *whole thing*, with the FELT SENSE of *all that*. Focusing helps the person to become aware of the whole thing *as a* whole. It enables people to work not just with various aspects of their concerns but with the concerns as wholes.

Part of the companion's role is to help the focuser to get to a place where they can sense the concern as a whole. Having browsed around in their feelings and thoughts and come to a concern that they wish to work with, the focuser tries to get a sense of 'all that issue'. The companion might invite the focuser to do just that. 'Can you sense it all as a whole? Can you feel it in your body? Where do you feel it?' As we have seen, people vary in how much they feel their concerns in their body and the companion may need to check with the focuser about the helpfulness of references to 'the body'.

Then, when the focuser has a FELT SENSE of the issue, the companion may help by reminding the focuser of the kinds of questions they might direct to the FELT SENSE. For example, 'You might like to ask what is really so bad about all this?' Or 'Perhaps you could now ask it what it needs?' If the focuser is already asking such questions then probably the companion need only listen.

There are practical issues about setting up focusing partnerships which are probably best to learn in a focusing workshop; for example, issues about personal boundaries, confidentiality, timekeeping, post-session discussion, and so on. The purpose of this chapter is not to explore such issues but to emphasise the interpersonal, interactive dimension of the practice. In focusing alone you are still engaged in this interactive kind of process but with yourself as a partner. In focusing alone you need to give to your own EXPERIENCING the friendly attention that a good focusing partner would give you, to remind yourself of what you might need to do, or to ask. Focusing alone is harder than focusing with a good focusing partner (though probably easier than doing it with a partner who is wrong for you!). It is harder, not simply for practical reasons, but because responding to oneself *really is* a more sophisticated activity than responding to another person. Interpersonal responses come first in human life, they are more basic: they are the foundation of our capacity to respond to ourselves.

The kind of thing that goes on in solitary focusing is one facet of what goes on in a focusing partnership. Now we can add that what goes on in a focusing partnership is one facet of a version of 'counselling'. To get a clearer view of what is involved in *this particular facet of counselling* we examined how it works in a focusing partnership. A focusing partnership session is rather *like* a counselling session but it doesn't have all the background and surroundings of counselling. It is just the focusing-interaction bit.

We began with solitary focusing and then looked at focusing partnerships. Now we need to put what we have learned about focusing partnerships back into the context in which focusing was first discovered—the context of counselling.

8

THE CORE OF
FOCUSING-ORIENTED COUNSELLING

One of the things that becomes clear from working in focusing partnerships is that the depth and effectiveness of the focusing process depends a great deal on the quality of the interaction between the focuser and the companion. Focusing usually works best where the companion is very *present* but does not *interfere*. It is this combination of supportive presence and openness to whatever comes that creates the safety needed in which the focuser can explore and CARRY FORWARD their EXPERIENCING. The first principle of F-OC, then, is that the therapist needs to do everything they can to create a friendly, interested, welcoming attitude towards whatever the client expresses. If the therapist senses that something is wrong in their interaction with the client then that needs attention before all else. For example, the client might be feeling that the therapist is more interested in getting them to focus than in listening to the story of their week. In this case it is crucial to let go of focusing and be with the client as they tell their story.

As with any form of counselling, the focusing-oriented counsellor has a theory about what may be helpful to the client. There is then the dilemma of whether the counsellor should primarily be guided by the theory or by what the client is saying. In F-OC the emphasis is on the client but that does not mean that the theory is irrelevant. As the counsellor works with the client the theory is there but it is IMPLICIT. It is present in the way that a violinist's knowledge of musical theory is present as they play. They do not think about the theory in the midst of the performance but their knowledge of the theory informs their playing. If something seems to be going wrong with their performance then the theory may come to mind and help them to correct their mistake, but the theory needs to be in the *background* if they are to play well (Polanyi, 1958).

So the counsellor's knowledge of the principles of focusing is there but IMPLICIT. Other aspects of their knowledge and experience will also be there IMPLICITLY—for example, all the other things they know about counselling as well as their own personal difficulties. At the start of the session the counsellor may consciously set aside their theoretical knowledge and their personal troubles and thereby clear a space within which they can receive the client. Later, they may need the things they have set aside— they can draw on their knowledge and on their own life experiences, but these things will be drawn out, if at all, in a way that is implicitly relevant to what is going on in the session. It is the interaction in the session that draws out relevant and freshly formulated aspects of the theory rather than the theory determining what should take place in the interaction.

The counsellor listens to the client, REFLECTING back as much as seems appropriate in order to maintain the connection with the client, to show them that what has been said has been understood and to begin the process of helping the client to 'listen' to their own EXPERIENCING. The counsellor needs to respond to what the client says in a way that encourages the client to sense their own feelings and responses. This is a delicate matter. On the one hand the counsellor does not want to direct the client—the change process needs to come from within the client; it needs to be *their* process. On the other hand the counsellor does want the client to find the source of possible change within themselves. So what is often helpful is some gentle encouragement in the direction of finding the inner places from which change might come.

One helpful kind of idea that might be in the back of the counsellor's mind would be to let the client tell their story but to watch out for those places where the client has some personal response to the events they are recalling; places where there is some poignancy, some stirring of feeling or emotion. By responding at these points the counsellor encourages the client to become a bit more aware of their feelings. Then the counsellor is happy for the client to continue with their story. When the client has settled in a bit more to the counselling process, the counsellor might make their interest in the client's feelings more EXPLICIT: 'You felt quite sad when she said that—could you just stay a minute with that sadness … what is it like … ?' This is in effect an invitation to the client to focus. The client might respond by saying 'I'm not sure what you mean—I just felt sad—wouldn't you?' Then the counsellor will probably drop their question and encourage the client to continue. But now they know that this client does not find it easy to stay with their feelings so that direct invitations to focus will not be helpful. They will continue to listen and reflect, sometimes responding a bit more at points where the client does express their feelings.

On the other hand the client may respond by saying, 'It's not an *awful* kind of sadness, but sort of deep … as if I've touched something deep down … .' The counsellor can sense here that the client is already focusing, so what is required is likely to be accurate and literal REFLECTION, 'It's as if you have touched something deep down.' Then the session may continue for several minutes in the sort of way that would be characteristic of a focusing partnership. Typically, the client experiences some FELT SHIFTS as they focus, new feelings emerge or a bit of new energy is released. The counsellor invites them to register the shifts, to feel the changed energy, to sense that something has moved a little. Then the client will continue with whatever comes next for them.

That is the sort of way in which focusing usually comes into F-OC. It is a gentle encouragement of a natural process rather than a teaching of the procedure. The reason for not teaching the procedure is that, in teaching, the teacher is active and oriented towards the content of what is to be taught. But, in counselling, it is crucial that the *client* should be active and that the counsellor should be oriented towards the client. The counselling process is one in which the counsellor supports, encourages and stimulates the LIFE-FORWARD movement (Gendlin, 1996, Chapter 20) of the client but does not determine it. This allows only a very limited role for teaching.

Teaching would be grounded in theory, and the place of theory in counselling is a delicate one. We have to avoid fitting the client into our theory and thus taking away from them their own unique perspective on their situation. On the other hand there are things we know about people and human situations that may be relevant. There has to be a constructive *interaction* between the general ideas of the theory and the particular and unique situation of the client. This is the philosophical issue from which focusing began: the interaction between general *concepts* and particular *experiences*. The creative interaction cannot take place if either side completely dominates the interaction. If the conceptual, COGNITIVE, theoretical side dominates then the client's unique EXPERIENCING is lost. Their experience simply becomes an illustration of the general concepts. If the unique, immediate, experiential side dominates then there can be no sense of patterns or meaning—just *this*. In many parts of our culture there is a bias towards the conceptual, and for this reason it can be important to give special emphasis to the unique EXPERIENCING of the client, but the creation of new meaning requires *both* staying with the EXPERIENCING *and* the trying out of new ways of formulating it in concepts or symbols.

In working with a client, the counsellor's theoretical knowledge should be 'in the background'. That means that it is there but not EXPLICIT. If the counsellor were thinking explicitly of the theory they could not give their full attention to the client, and if they were guided EXPLICITLY by the theory they would not be in a creative interaction with the client. Nevertheless, the theory informs what the counsellor says and does. They would say and do rather different things had they not learned the theory. What the theory says may be *relevant* to what the client says but just how it is relevant is determined by the client's situation not by the theory. No theory can specify in advance how one should act in a situation but the theory may draw our attention to things we might have missed without it. The role of theory in counselling is to *SENSITISE* us to possibilities of response that could be helpful to the client.

Focusing theory makes us especially sensitive to the importance of the client's EXPERIENCING, and to the ways in which we might respond so that the client's EXPERIENCING is carried forward rather than shut down. We will look at some of these ways in the rest of this chapter.

The central issue in F-OC is to find ways of responding to the client that will help the client to find their *own* ways of responding.

The counsellor's responses need to 'point' to the client's own EXPERIENCING (Gendlin, 1968). It is as if we are saying, 'Don't (primarily) listen to what the books say, don't listen to what other people say, don't even listen to what I say—except this—listen to your own EXPERIENCING.' REFLECTION is employed a lot in F-OC in order to point at the client's EXPERIENCING. It is a little different from 'just saying it back' and also a bit different from showing that you have understood. The point of this sort of REFLECTING is to help the client stay with their EXPERIENCING in a way that helps forward steps to come from the EXPERIENCING. The client says, 'I don't know … I feel so sad'—in connection with the end of their relationship. This could simply be said back: 'You feel so sad'. If the client were already on the edge of focusing this could be just what was needed. They hear their own words back and can sense whether those words are still just right. Expressing something, formulating it in words, *changes* it. At the very least it is now an expressed feeling rather than an unexpressed feeling. So when the client hears back, even the *exact* words they have said, they may now want to say something different, something more: '… not exactly sad … but kind of resigned'. 'Sad' *was* the right word but now it is not. *In* the feeling that was expressed by 'sad' there is much *more*—there, but IMPLICIT. The REFLECTION by the counsellor helps the client to make this *more* EXPLICIT. That is a little therapeutic step or MOMENT OF MOVEMENT.

However, it may be that when the client says, 'I feel so sad' they are *not* at the edge of focusing—not, that is, sensing the whole feel of their situation. Instead, their EXPERIENCING is narrowed down to 'I'm just sad—who wouldn't be?' In this situation, if the therapist REFLECTS, 'You are sad' the client may feel irritated. 'Yes, I am sad—I just told you. The point is what do I do about it? I shouldn't still be sad after all this time.' Here, where the client has the emotion but no FELT SENSE of their situation, the task of the counsellor is to help the client to regain such a FELT SENSE. The counsellor knows (here is the theory) that no-one is ever 'just sad': the sadness is an aspect of a whole situation, it is *this* person's response to all that which happened last year and all that that meant, all that it connects with from the more distant past, the disappointed hopes, the unfairness of it. *All that*, which goes far beyond anything that could be expressed in words. There *is* an *all that*, but the client has no *sense* of *all that*, just the feeling that she calls 'sad' and which she wants to escape from. Just staying with the 'sad' is unlikely to help—the client will simply feel *more* sad! What is needed is for the counsellor to 'point to' what lies around the sadness. The counsellor might say, 'What is it like to be so sad?' or 'What does this sadness do to you?' The client might just respond with 'I don't know, I'm just sad', and then the counsellor needs to come back to where the client was and say something like 'Ok—that question wasn't helpful … you were saying you wanted to get rid of the sadness … .' But often a client will respond more positively to the counsellor's 'POINTING':

> T: What does this sadness do to you?
> C: It makes me feel frustrated.
> T: Frustrated …
> C: It makes me angry … I'm angry with myself for being like this.
> T: There's something really angry there—anger with yourself.
> C: And not just with myself—I'm angry with *him.*
> T: In this anger there are two bits … anger at yourself and anger at him … maybe you could just sense both of those for a minute … and then see which needs your attention most … anger at yourself … anger at him …
> C: It's the anger at him that I'm really feeling now.
> T: You are angry with *him*. What would you like to say to him?

Here there have already been several steps. In the *all that* of the client's situation there are facets of frustration and of two kinds of anger. These were not EXPLICIT when she said, 'I'm just sad' but they were 'there' in the way that so much *is* IMPLICITLY there in a situation. In her stuck situation there is no way forward if she simply labels her feeling as 'sad'—in order to move forward she has to dip down into what is 'under' or 'around' the 'sad'. Then new facets of the situation emerge, which often have some potential to *change* the situation. The client doesn't *want* to be the way she is, so that the new facets that emerge are likely to be helpful rather than irrelevant. What emerges is to some extent 'selected' by the felt needs of the client from all the myriad things that *could* emerge.

The aspect of F-OC that we have been looking at in this chapter is closely related to what goes on in a focusing-partnership session. But much of F-OC is not so much 'focusing' as an *orienting towards* focusing. Often, clients are not in touch with their EXPERIENCING or have no FELT SENSE of their difficulties, or they have come to a point where they need to CARRY FORWARD in some other way what has come in a FELT SHIFT. There are phases of F-OC which lead up to focusing and phases that lead away from it. We will look at this in the next chapter.

9

HELPING THE CLIENT RELATE
TO THEIR EXPERIENCING

The core pattern of F-OC is that the client begins with an issue which they may formulate in various ways, for instance in terms of certain ideas (e.g. 'I am not assertive enough and I want to change'), or images ('I feel that my relationship has become a cage'), or emotions ('I always seem to be anxious at present'), or sensations ('I feel sick whenever I have to go to those meetings'). The counsellor listens and responds in a way that helps the client to appreciate that they are being taken seriously. A basic trust is established and this needs to be maintained throughout the sessions. Some clients then naturally begin to focus with their problems so that they move from the initial formulations to a deeper FELT-SENSE level from which change-steps can come. In this case the counsellor needs to do little but accompany them. Other clients do not engage so naturally with their EXPERIENCING and then the counsellor needs to make moves that will help them to do so. In this limited sense F-OC is 'directive'—it gently encourages the client to relate to their own EXPERIENCING and their potential for forward movement.

There are many different ways in which clients can find it difficult to relate creatively to their EXPERIENCING and so there are many ways in which the counsellor can be of help. But each client is different and what helps with one client may not help with the next. It is the counsellor's FELT SENSE of the therapeutic situation which needs to determine how they respond and which aspect of their experience and knowledge they can best draw upon. With that important qualification we will now look at some of the possible ways of helping.

CLEARING A SPACE

Sometimes a client comes with a long list of difficulties. They are anxious and panicky because their partner is threatening to leave but also because they are about to start a new and unfamiliar job; the mortgage is in arrears; they are being criticised by their mother for not getting a grip on their life; their child is ill and there is another one on the way … it is OVERWHELMING. The anxiety and panic attacks are being fed from many sources, each of which needs attention. But the client cannot get a sense of the way forward with any of the difficulties because the anxiety from all the others interferes. Here it may help for the counsellor to suggest something like the pre-focusing procedure of 'clearing a space'. It has the two aspects of separating the concerns and of getting a bit of distance from them. So the counsellor might say something about how they see the initial difficulty of being overwhelmed and then suggest that the client give some attention to each issue—enough to feel it as a 'whole thing' but not so much that they start going into it and trying to sort it out. Can they be aware of it—'all that thing' and then stand back a bit from it or set it down a little way away? Have a short holiday from it? Then the same with the other issues, followed by a bit of time to feel the relief of not being completely submerged by the problems. Then the question of which of the problems is most pressing. Can the others wait for a little? Sometimes people do this sort of thing spontaneously. A client says, 'I put each of my problems in a drawer and lock it— apart from that problem with my brother; *that* drawer won't close!'

Both in the focusing procedure and in counselling this 'space clearing' is a preliminary practice—it can get a person to a place where they can begin to work with an issue.

'TOO CLOSE' AND 'TOO FAR'

Being overwhelmed by emotion is one thing that can prevent a client from engaging with their EXPERIENCING. They are *too close* to their feelings. It is in this sort of situation that the focusing *moves* of 'standing back a bit', 'putting it down', 'making a space for it' can be very valuable. But it is not a matter of automatically trying these things when a client is EMOTIONALLY OVERWHELMED. It may be more important to let the client know that you are there, that you are trying to understand. The client may need to be 'held' while they go through their emotion. Or the client may feel so vulnerable that they can't even begin to talk about the issue until they feel absolutely certain they will not be rejected. The interpersonal context comes first, then listening and receiving. Focusing and approaches to focusing come *third*, not first.

If the initial difficulty with some clients is that they are 'too close' to their feelings, with others the problem is that they are 'too far' from them. Here we have the kinds of difficulty discussed earlier where a client talks about their situation in a purely intellectual way, or talks about events in their life without referring to how things struck them or how they felt about them. Similarly with clients who talk about what they are doing, or might do, to 'fix' their problems, without pausing to sense what the heart of the problem really is. I described the focusing-oriented approach to this sort of difficulty earlier: one stays with the client, but gently pauses at the places where there is some connection with feeling.

INNER CRITICS

It is hard to explore one's EXPERIENCING if one does not feel safe. That is partly why Rogers' 'CORE CONDITIONS' are so important in counselling. But even if the counsellor is accepting of everything that the client says, the *client* may not have that attitude. Often when new thoughts or feelings begin to emerge, something in the client rejects them as 'silly', or 'impractical' or 'wrong'. It seems to be part of human nature that we subject ourselves to inner criticism and, in a way, that is healthy and useful. When we have an impulse to do something it is often just as well that we should pause and consider the whole context: 'Do I really want to do that?' But this part of our normal functioning can become rigid and punishing. Rather than raising a *question* about what we are feeling it condemns it out of hand with phrases such as 'That's just stupid!' or 'You couldn't possibly do that!'. It is as if we are in the presence of a highly directive and authoritarian 'counsellor' who is not at all interested in listening to us. That part of us may be experienced almost as an inner voice—often it has the tone of a critical parent—or it may be present more by way of a sinking or constricting feeling that arises when we come to a particular bit of our EXPERIENCING. It can be hard and controlling ('That's just not good enough!') or soft and manipulative ('You wouldn't want to do *that*, would you?').

This sort of critical 'voice' is known as the 'INNER CRITIC' although sometimes it might be better described as an inner 'saboteur' or 'wet blanket'. Where such a part of us is active it will be difficult for us to focus, so something needs to be done about the critic. There are two complementary approaches (Gendlin, 1978/2003, 1996, Chapter 19; Cornell, 2005, pp. 105–25; Stinckens et al., 2002). The short-term way is to wave the critic off. For example:

C: I just had a strange idea—I'd like to learn to *sail.*
T: Something in you says you'd like to learn to sail.
C: Yes … but that's silly—I'm much too clumsy—I'd make a complete mess of it.
T: There's something there saying you'd make a mess of it, but can we put that aside for a minute? *You* were saying you'd like to learn to sail …

This is like stopping a person from interrupting an important conversation. We don't need to attack them for interrupting but they need to be *stopped* or else something important will be lost.

Sometimes the INNER CRITIC refuses to be stopped and then we need to relate to *it* before returning to what the client was saying. The counsellor can help the client to dialogue with the critical voice (we will look at such a dialogue below) and what often happens then is that the critical voice softens while the client becomes stronger. *Then* the client can return to where they were before the critical attack. In the longer term this is probably the best way to work with inner critics.

DIVIDED EXPERIENCING

There are many situations in which clients are divided in their EXPERIENCING (Greenberg et al., 1993, Chapter 10; Gendlin, 1996,

Chapter 13; Mearns & Thorne, 1988/2007, pp. 33–5; Cornell & McGavin, 2002, pp. 155–86). The client says that they want to leave their job but they can't because of their fear of what their family will say. As the counsellor helps them to stay with *all that* about leaving, the other bit chips in with why they *can't* leave. But if the counsellor then follows the client's feelings about not being able to leave, the wanting-to-leave bit reasserts itself. The client cannot go far into either aspect of their EXPERIENCING because the other 'part' of them blocks the process. This is a place where a GESTALT counsellor might use a two-chair procedure. The counsellor pulls up another chair and gets the client to role-play the two parts while sitting in the different chairs. This helps to separate the parts. While in one chair the client can really feel one side of their dilemma and in the other chair they can feel the other side. Focusing-oriented counsellors occasionally use this procedure, but it introduces an unnecessarily directive element into the counselling situation (though drama students may like it!). Rather than drawing up the extra chair the counsellor can simply encourage the two sides to speak in turn. The following dialogue will illustrate this as well as providing an example of relating to a critical voice:

> T: You'd really like to learn to sail …
> C: Yes, it's an exciting idea, but—
> T: There's something there that objects … can we hear what it has to say?
> C: It says—sailing may be an exciting idea but it's stupid and a waste of money. It's not the sort of thing you are good at. You'd make a fool of yourself and probably put other people in danger. It's just not your sort of thing.
> T: How do you respond to *that*?
> C: Well it's true really. I *am* pretty useless at physical things.
> T: How does that make you feel?
> C: Sort of sad, not allowed to do things that other people do.
> T: So what does the other bit say about that?
> C: It says … I'm just trying to be realistic—I'm not trying to hurt you … but clumsy people shouldn't go sailing!

T: And is that OK?

C: No—That still makes me feel bad … There's something not right here … I'm not *always* clumsy and people *can* learn things if they take time … and there are people who will help.

T: What does the other one say to that?

C: It's a bit grumpy and it says something like … You'd really have to do this properly. You'd have to have sailing lessons … I suppose you could try it … then you'll see it isn't for you.

T: And what do you say to that?

C: OK—so I *will* try it.

T: You might like to take a minute to sense how all that feels now …

C: It feels … sort of released … a bit scary … but a feeling of there's no going back …

Here both sides get to express their feelings and, as a result, the timid side becomes stronger and the critical side (a bit!) more flexible. Now it is possible for the client to take an ACTION STEP, which will probably have implications that go well beyond this particular difficulty.

At the end of the dialogue the counsellor may need to bring the client back to how the whole situation now feels. The dialogue itself is not a focusing procedure, but focusing can take place within it, and focusing may also arise at the end as the client senses how their feelings have changed and what might be the next step forward.

SUPPRESSED EXPERIENCING

Sometimes parts or aspects of us are suppressed and remain IMPLICIT because they would give rise to severe anxiety if they became EXPLICIT (Greenberg et al.. 1993, Chapter 11; Gendlin, 1996, Chapter 13). This is the territory of 'REPRESSION'. What is EXPLICIT is a feeling of constriction or heaviness, for example, but it is not clear what is causing these feelings. The focusing-oriented approach is to help the client to stay close to the feelings and to sense the whole situation that is being registered as 'tight' or 'heavy'. The counsellor might say, 'There is something sitting heavily on you … can you get a sense of that *something*?'. The word 'something' is a very valuable word in F-OC—it *points* without imposing any particular content. The client will provide the content. The counsellor may need to keep up a kind of gentle 'patter'—'There's that heavy thing … let's just sit with it a bit … is that OK for it? … it is *heavy* … we are just being with it … can you get a sense of what sort of *heavy* this is? …'. Then something may come—a thought, or an image, or a memory. Perhaps the client now says that she has an image of a great bird perched on her shoulders, holding her down. 'There's a big bird on my shoulders … I can feel its weight … .' The counsellor suggests that the client lets herself really feel the weight of the bird—it is *so heavy*. At this point the source of the heaviness has become explicit to some extent but, as yet, it is just an image. The counsellor then encourages the client to stay with the image. Can she describe the bird? What is it like? *It is like a great eagle.* Now can the client get a fuller sense of the eagle—what would it be like to be this eagle? *Oh, the eagle is strong, perceptive, powerful … .* The counsellor encourages the client to feel this strength and power. It is as if the client can to some extent *be* the eagle. Then the client can begin to get a sense of what the eagle is doing. It is keeping *a tight grip* on the client … making sure that she sees exactly what is going on so that no one can deceive or manipulate her … .

At this point a new aspect or part of the client has become EXPLICIT. The client's EXPERIENCING is no longer just that of the person who feels the heaviness or the tight grip. What is *making* the heaviness is now EXPLICIT to some extent. Now that both parts are EXPLICIT the client can work with either of them but especially with *all that* which has been making her feel heavy and constricted. *All that* has an unfamiliar strength and energy in it—and, of course, this may be of great value to the client if she can become more in touch with it.

CURTAILED EXPERIENCING

From a focusing-oriented point of view, organic life is a process, a becoming, a CARRYING-FORWARD. For human beings this CARRYING-FORWARD is often a matter of expressing, of SYMBOLISING in words, or images, or movements. When what is IMPLICIT is CARRIED FORWARD and becomes EXPLICIT there is a sense of flow and freedom—now the next thing can come. However, this flow can be interrupted or blocked. That often happens with traumatic events. What would or should have come—tears, anger, flight—couldn't come because of the situation the person was in. They couldn't cry because they were expected to be 'strong', they couldn't shout and scream because that would have made things worse, they couldn't run away because there was nowhere to go. In such situations what is IMPLICIT is not CARRIED-FORWARD in the normal way. But it is, in another way, CARRIED-FORWARD—it is carried in the form of a blockage that is held in the body.

The expression of feeling can be blocked by circumstances other than obvious trauma, but the broad pattern is the same—the expression has been curtailed and the emotion remains IMPLICIT until something can be done that enables it to CARRY FORWARD properly into speech or action. This is often called 'UNFINISHED BUSINESS' or 'CATHARSIS'. In F-OC the counsellor provides a safe place for CATHARSIS and welcomes whatever needs to come, but does not seek to 'pull out' such emotions. The emotion needs to come naturally from the place where it has been blocked. The frozen place needs to thaw and part of the counsellor's task is to provide the warmth that will encourage the thawing.

Where EXPERIENCING has been curtailed it loses its natural life and flow. In Gendlin's (1964/1973) phrase it becomes 'STRUCTURE-BOUND'. There is no longer EXPERIENC*ING* (the creative interplay between feeling and meaning) but just a fixed, frozen experience. The client can't interact with their frozen experience and nor can the counsellor. Instead the counsellor needs to interact with what is around and close to the frozen place but is not itself frozen. The client themselves will probably keep away from this adjacent area (that is why nothing changes) but the counsellor can gently interact with what is there.

For example, in the case of the client situation discussed in the previous chapter the client's sadness may have a frozen quality to it. The counsellor tries to find ways of talking around the sadness—'When you are out with your friends, do you feel sad then?' 'No, but as soon as I come home I'm sad again. It's always there.' Or 'You are sad because your friend went away—but don't you also feel a bit resentful?' 'No ... I just feel sad.' There may be no way forward from here, at least for the moment, but questions such as the one previously suggested may draw a response: 'What is it like being always sad like this?' This invites the client to step away a little from the sadness and reflect on it from a place close by. In the case described, the client now says it is *frustrating* and, when this is REFLECTED, she says she is angry. Here we see her EXPERIENCING restored; here there is interaction between the concepts and the experiences. As she stays with the anger it becomes differentiated into anger at herself and anger at her friend; there is a CARRYING-FORWARD. Here, quite close to the 'frozen', sad place is a place where she is *not* frozen. It is not a place that she naturally goes to because she has deep fears about getting angry, but in the safe atmosphere of the counselling session she can go there. The *anger* is not frozen, it is alive, but it is connected with the frozen sadness. Now she explores the anger a bit and becomes aware of a fear that tends to suppress it. This brings back memories of how her father used to get angry with her, of how she tried not to do anything that made him angry ... but also ... the sadness of not being able to be close to him ... she begins to experience *that* sadness ... the tears come ... it was so *sad* that they couldn't be close ... *This* sadness is alive—not at all frozen. It connects spontaneously with other feelings for, and memories of, her father. Then when she comes back to her feelings for her friend the sadness is still there but it is different. The sadness about her father flows into *this* sadness, and this sadness connects to her father and his anger and *all that* about never getting angry. The sad place is no longer frozen.

Further discussion of 'curtailed EXPERIENCING' can be found in Greenberg et al. (1993, Chapter 12), Gendlin (1996, Chapter

16), and Goldman (2002). The more traumatic varieties of curtailed EXPERIENCING need much more discussion than is appropriate here. There is a developing body of knowledge about trauma that has deep and interesting connections with focusing. A good introduction to this area can be found in Peter Levine (1997) and Babette Rothschild (2000). The special difficulties and dangers of working with traumatised clients are things that all counsellors should be aware of, regardless of their theoretical orientation.

CONSTRUALS AND STRUCTURE-BOUND EXPERIENCING

According to focusing theory there are always two inputs into our EXPERIENCING—there are the immediate and particular feelings and there is what comes from our general understanding and knowledge. These two inputs can be separated in thought but in practice they come together. For example, someone has left their mobile phone on the counselling-room table. We see it there and this involves experiences of colour and shape but also experiences of uncertainty about whose it is and anxiety that it may ring during the session. Those are particular experiences but they are formulated in general concepts, the concepts of colour, shape, uncertainty, anxiety, mobile phone. Someone unfamiliar with mobile phones wouldn't have some of these experiences; they wouldn't even see the object as a mobile phone. The experience of the thing on the table would not carry them forward in the same way.

One way of saying this is that in our EXPERIENCING there are always *CONSTRUALS* of what is there, of what the situation is. These CONSTRUALS come partly from the immediate EXPERIENCING and partly from the concepts that we bring to the EXPERIENCING. The *balance* between these two is important. If we are unable to bring our concepts to bear effectively on the situation, because we are tired or drunk, for example, then our EXPERIENCING is likely to be confusing and frightening. But conversely, we can be so much under the sway of our general concepts and expectations that we hardly notice how *this* situation does not fit them. Ideally, EXPERIENCING is an interplay between what 'is there' and what we would expect. Each of these modifies the other—our direct experience of the person modifies our stereotyped conception of them but also our general understanding of people enables us to see aspects of this person that we would not otherwise have seen.

Difficulties arise when we are CARRIED-FORWARD too exclusively by our direct awareness or too exclusively by our expectations. The first situation can generate chaos while the second can lead to our being caught in old patterns. It is the second situation that can be called 'misconstrued EXPERIENCING'. It is the situation where, instead of giving our attention freshly to what is happening, our EXPERIENCING is CARRIED-FORWARD mostly by our *ideas* about it, by what we would usually expect. We don't see the shyness of the psychiatrist or of the head teacher because we are CARRIED-FORWARD not by *them* but by our pattern of reactions to people whom we categorise as authority figures. We are STRUCTURE-BOUND—living in our general conceptions rather relating these freshly to the new particular encounter.

In some schools of therapy this situation would be described as one in which we are not being 'rational'. It is not *reasonable* to think that head teachers can't be shy and so we need to modify our irrational thinking. The focusing-oriented perspective is different. It is not a matter of modifying irrational thinking—after all, who is to say for sure what counts as rational? (Clearly, we couldn't apply some of *our* standards of rationality to cultures in which magic plays a significant role.) The difficulty is not about rationality, in the sense of whether we see things as they 'objectively' are, but of whether we can allow our general conceptions and understandings to be modified by our encounter with the situation.

The point is not so much that we 'misconstrue', in the sense of getting it wrong, but that we are not sufficiently open to whether our CONSTRUAL is a helpful one. PROCESS-EXPERIENTIAL THERAPY (Greenberg et al., 1993; Elliott et al., 2004) approaches misconstruals through giving attention to the 'dysfunctional EMOTION SCHEMES' that are held to lie behind them, but the notion of 'dysfunctional emotion' is problematical. What seems dysfunctional to the counsellor may not be dysfunctional for the client. Especially in cross-cultural work, it is risky to make firm assumptions about which emotions are 'normal' and which are 'dysfunctional'. The important thing is what carries the client forward. The only *general* thing we can say is that, to the extent that the client's EXPERIENCING is STRUCTURE-BOUND, to *that* extent they will not be able to interact effectively with other people or with the rest of the world and, hence, will not be able to CARRY FORWARD in any full way.

The general way of working with STRUCTURE-BOUND EXPERIENCING is that which we discussed in connection with curtailed EXPERIENCING. When EXPERIENCING is curtailed the problem is precisely that it tends to become STRUCTURE-BOUND. The counsellor can't work directly with the 'frozen' structure but they can work with EXPERIENCING that is close to it. Then the structure can begin to soften.

This chapter has presented a variety of things that can interfere with a client's capacity to relate to their EXPERIENCING. There are other difficulties of this kind, some of which can be found in the writings of the PROCESS-EXPERIENTIAL therapists. They are things to be sensitive to, but it is not a matter of simply spotting the difficulty and then applying the procedure. The focusing-oriented counsellor tries to be sensitive to the whole person and to how things are in the client–therapist relationship. It is only within that context that the counsellor and client may find that certain procedures are nevertheless of great value.

10

A FOCUSING-ORIENTED COUNSELLING
TRANSCRIPT

As should be clear by now, there can be several different phases in a focusing-oriented counselling session. Much of the session can involve helping the client to feel safe and accepted; simply listening to the client and REFLECTING the more important or poignant aspects of what the client says. The other, more specifically focusing-oriented responses, may occupy a relatively small part of the session. And often the client will move naturally between focusing and talking in a more ordinary way.

In the following session the client has some familiarity with focusing and finds it a natural thing to do. Since listening and reflecting are better known than focusing-oriented responses, I have selected two segments from the recording of the session in which focusing-oriented responses predominate. There are probably more of them than there usually would be in a typical F-OC session.

The client, whom I will call Andrew, begins by speaking of a kind of discomfort he sometimes feels with people and mentions a recent situation in which this happened. He also says that it might actually happen in the session and he would be glad if it did happen. Then it occurs to him that the same sort of thing can happen when he is reading a book:

A1: … So in my mind, sitting here sort of reflecting on it, it's as if there is a boxing ring, for example … and it's *oppositional*. That's what I get.

C1: It's oppositional …

A2: So the words on the page—or spoken—the hostility—is sort of an oppositional-ness … why would I want to do that?

C2: Well, maybe we will get to that … but that catches it pretty well? It's an opposition …

His question seems to take him away from his EXPERIENCING. If he pursues it I suspect that he will lose touch with the feel *of 'oppositional-ness', just as a client can easily lose touch with what they are feeling if the* counsellor *asks them* why *they are feeling it. So I let the question go by and respond instead to the 'feel'.*

A3: Mm.

C3: If someone says something, then there's an opposing of that.

A4: Yes.

C4: A not-letting-it-come-in. 'This is me … keep back'.

I am trying out various formulations. It doesn't matter so much whether they are 'right'. Their function is more to help the client stay with his EXPERIENCING *as he checks it against them.*

A5: Mm.

C5: There is a resisting.

I put it like this, rather than as 'You are resisting it' so as to help him notice the feel *of the resisting rather than simply resisting.*

A6: Yeah, yes … *I'm doing it here.* I'm wondering how does it feel to me now to hear you say these words.

The issue is already arising here, in the session.

C6: Yes.

A7: Because in a way that's it. I'm trying to meet you or I'm not trying to meet you, or something like that.

C7: Something like that. It's happening sort of here.

A8: Yeah … So when you said 'resisting something' I feel like I'm resisting something in myself, as opposed to resisting you, although I do feel like I can … it's strange … I got the sense that again it's a fear, or something, that I'm resisting … In here. I'm keeping it down.

A FELT SENSE *begins to form: notice the 'something'. There is the resisting, he can sense it, he gets a glimpse of* what *he is resisting. Then it is more a 'keeping it down'. There are several small* FELT SHIFTS *here.*

C8:   You're keeping it down. So perhaps we need to ack-
        nowledge there's that fear …
*This is to ensure that we don't lose the new thing that has come—
the fear. Actually I have been a bit too definite here: he said only
'it's a fear,' or something'.*

A9:   Yes.
C9:   Something like a *fear*.
I try to pick up my 'mistake' in C8.

A10: *Yes.* [emphatically]
C10: There's a fear there that maybe you are keeping down.
*I take it that his emphatic response does confirm that it really is
fear, but I could be wrong about that.*

A11: Yeah … Yeah …
C11: So I want to say—let's make a bit of space for that fear, so
        it can be there —
*This is a mini-version of 'clearing a space'. Andrew is sufficiently
familiar with focusing to understand what it means. With another
client I might need to explain a bit what I am suggesting here.*

A12: Yeah.
C12: There's some fear there.
A13: I'm feeling there—I'm trying to sense that. Gosh! *It's there*
        …
Here is a FELT SHIFT in which there is no change in the content, *but
the client newly appreciates the* strength *of the feeling.*

C13: Can we sort of be in touch with that fear without getting—
*I was going to say 'without getting drawn into it'. This is to help
the client to keep at the right distance from the emotion. I have
probably said this sort of thing several times in earlier sessions.
Andrew knows what I am going to say before I say it!*

A14: Yes, kind of. I'm getting things like … I've come across it
        before. It's like a nervousness or a butterfly-iness. In a

faint sense I feel it at the moment.

C14: Just faint—butterfly-y.

This is the very straight sort of REFLECTION *that is appropriate when the client is focusing.*

A15: Yes, and the tension here that it gives me.

C15: All that.

I'm encouraging him to stay with the whole of it.

A16: It's an itchiness as well … I get itchy.

C16: 'Itchy' is a good word for it.

A17: Mm.

C17: It's itchy.

A18: Oh, yes … No … what you say—*it* is itchy. I was going to say 'No, it's me that's itchy', but no, *it* is itchy.

Here Andrew spontaneously makes the distinction between 'him' *and* 'it'.

C18: It is itchy—so we are here sort of … looking at it, and it is itchy.

It can help to say 'we' rather than 'you' so that the client doesn't feel alone with their feeling.

A19: Yes.

C19: Right.

A20: It's an 'embarrassing' as well, actually. I've felt that before … it's a terribly unconfident-ness … that can feel embarrassed …

As he stays with 'it' new facets emerge.

C20: Well I guess we need to go a bit gently with it … It's embarrassed … to show itself? … Can you still sense it there?

Where there is embarrassment it can be hard for the next thing to come. I want to check that the embarrassment hasn't pushed the FELT SENSE *away.*

A21: Now it is more 'frustrated'.

C21: Frustrated …

A22: I feel like I've retreated now.

It seems that the embarrassment has interfered.

C22: You have come way back from it.

A23: Or back from you.

Here is a new twist that connects again with what he said at the start about the possibility of the difficulty happening in the session.

C23: Or from me.

A24: Yes.

C24: Maybe I've been pushing a little bit much.

I want him to know that I would be happy to respond in a different way if that would help.

A25: Or … um … mm … ah … it's … um … ah … no … well there's such a safety for me in retreating from you or … from going at it with you here … it's such an easy place to go … but, um … I can disengage and disappear almost at any moment with people … And that's partly what I meant about not being well adapted to social situations sometimes. The disappearing. I'm not *there* any more. Um.

Now another new facet emerges—he is concerned about his disengaging or disappearing.

C25: Yeah.

A26: And I think I used to appear quite morose, but I don't do that any more. I can still disappear but I don't have this cloud over my head …

C26: You can *quietly* disappear [both laugh].

A27: Yeah.

C27: And I don't know that I mind that … what is it that troubles me? … the trouble is that I have a sense that I am blocking myself or inhibiting myself … the other day—this is where my mind's gone—at work there's a bit of bother —

He has come to a block or disengagement, here in the session. He perhaps senses that it is time to take a break from focusing and moves into talking about recent events at work. I am happy to follow him in this. He talks about some of his feelings and relationships at work and how in various spots in his life there is some kind of blocking ...

C28: All this is centring round this blocking ...

I sense that it might be helpful to pick up on the 'all this' which he has been describing. This is in effect an invitation to focus again. He may or may not take it up.

    A28: Yes. I block myself or ... it's insidious and so *familiar* that I can't see what I am doing.

    C29: Mm.

    A29: And that is a little bit frustrating sitting *here*—I can feel my self ... like a ball of string that's tied up. I want to pull it, but I know if I do it will knot.

    C30: If you pull it, it will just make it worse.

    A30: Yeah. Yeah. Yeah.

    C31: OK—so it's not good to pull it ... too tight ... it's all tangled ...

    A31: Yeah. Yeah ... I feel like I'm searching. And I feel like I do that here. I feel like I'm doing that all day. Searching for something ... and it's funny—[Client indicates his head.]

For Andrew there is a difference between the sort of thinking that goes on 'up there'—'in the head' and a more BODILY SENSE of the issue.

    C32: It's going on up here—more than—

    A32: It can do. Yeah, you're absolutely right.

    C33: Perhaps you could let it come down a bit ... so there's a bit more of a physical sense of this tangly thing.

It can often help to feel the issue in the central part of the body. Of course not all clients would understand this sort of talk without some explanation.

A33: Mm …

C34: Can you get a feel of what it needs … what would be helpful … or … ?

This is a use of one of the alternative focusing questions. It may or may not help.

A34: It needs to be balanced … I feel unbalanced by it.

C35: There's an *unbalanced* …

This doesn't catch all of what he has said. I miss the need *to be balanced.*

A35: It's only knotted because I go at it so fast or hard … It's edgy …

Because of this, perhaps, he stays with how it is rather than with what is needed.

C36: Edgy.

Again I miss an important part of what he has said—that it's knotted because he goes at it so fast or hard.

A36: Yeah.

C37: It might be more helpful to be more gentle or something like that?

I am responding now to what I missed in C36. In F-OC the counsellor often *'makes mistakes'. That is not something to be very upset about—one simply does one's best to rectify them.*

A37: Exactly. Gentle … where is my gentleness? … You know what … the answer came back … 'It's mixed up.' My gentleness is next to my sadness, or my … yeah … it is …

This is a striking example of what Gendlin calls 'the body talking back'. His FELT SENSE tells him how things are.

C38: The gentleness and the sadness are really close.

A38: They are. It's hard to get to the gentleness—it brings the sadness with it.

C39: Yes.

A39: That's weird … huh … or maybe it isn't … *[sighs]* …

C40: It's really hard to separate the gentleness from the sadness …

A40: It is … it's the … well … it's compassion that I need for myself … that when I get the hostility and the oppositional- ness that's exactly what I haven't found—where I'm not at …

From his expression it is clear that something is happening in Andrew. I don't know what it is.

A41: That's weird—the sensation I just felt. Um … um … like I'd been hit on the back of the head. Like you get a moment's concussion if you bang your head—just a split second … that was really strange, that was so strange. My word …

C41: As if you were hit there.

A42: Yeah it did. I had so many thoughts going through my head at the same time, and they all link.

C42: Mmm.

There are always many interconnected things in what comes in a shift such as this. I feel it is best just to wait and see what happens next …

A43: I long to be happy with my sadness, but I'm not. I resist it—I don't want it. It's strange—with all the work that we've come through it's still this residue of not wanting it. And by not wanting it I feel it's hard to get to the gentleness, especially once I get into an oppositional frame of mind.

C43: Mm.

A44: And I dissect people … the being held back … the un- comfortableness … I don't need to be like that … such a strain on me.

C44: It's a real strain … It's this thing of not wanting the sadness … which tangles things up.

A45: Yeah … I know that I need to learn to be gentle with myself … but for so long I've not done that and I don't know … truly how to be that gentleness …

C45: Something you've never … done?

A46: I can do—I have done it—I know it when I come here, or in certain therapy situations when I get really into myself … then I feel such compassion towards other people and towards myself.

C46: Ah … yes.

A47: Such a gentleness.

C47: Yeah.

A48: It's something else. It really is.

He means it 'really is something important', not that it is literally another thing. The session comes to an end soon after this. There have been many steps, he has got to something deeply important to him—his gentleness, and he knows that it can be hard to get to the gentleness because it brings with it a sadness. More steps may later come from here.

11

GLIMPSES OF A THEORY

Most people come to focusing either as a self-help practice or as an important element in their counselling practice. They find that it 'works' or is helpful and do not raise the question of how it works, or why it is helpful. There is nothing wrong with that—it is not necessary to understand how focusing works in order to benefit from it, any more than it is necessary to know how a television works in order to enjoy watching it.

On the other hand it is reasonable to ask what the justification is for practising a particular form of counselling, or indeed for practising counselling at all. One sort of justification comes through collecting empirical evidence that counselling (or focusing) is effective. I will discuss that approach in the next chapter, but there is another sort of justification, which is a matter of showing how the effectiveness of a form of therapy *follows from* more general considerations about human nature or about the world as a whole. Theories are developed in order to provide such a general background to practice. But they can also be practically useful because, if something goes wrong in practice, we naturally ask 'Why?' and the theory may suggest an answer. It may also provide some ideas about how the difficulty might be resolved. Theory need not be remote from practice—a good theory connects strongly with practice.

The theory at the back of focusing has been developed mainly by Gendlin (1962/1997, 1964b/1973, 1990, 1991, 1997) over a period of about forty years. I can give only some glimpses of it here, but I hope I can say enough to indicate its relevance not only to focusing and counselling but also to much wider issues. (It is possible, of course, that alternative theories may be developed in order to explain focusing—what we know about the effectiveness of focusing is independent of Gendlin's theory.)

Focusing grew up in the broad tradition of HUMANISTIC COUNSELLING and this form of counselling faces serious challenges in the contemporary climate of opinion. That climate is infused with a way of thinking that emphasises what is EXPLICIT, rule-governed, quantifiable. In this context people speak of the dominance of the 'MEDICAL MODEL' with its emphasis on techniques. Many counsellors (and others) are deeply opposed to the model but they do not have a well-worked-out alternative with which to combat it.

What Gendlin does is to provide such an alternative model (Gendlin 1997). This is a large task because the roots of the 'MEDICAL MODEL' go back a long way. The story begins in the seventeenth century with what has been called 'the MECHANISATION of the world picture' (Dijksterhuis, 1961). The work of philosophers and scientists such as Galileo, Descartes and Newton led to a picture of the world that was atomistic, deterministic, and quantifiable. The picture was so successful that it soon ceased to be regarded as a picture or model but was taken to constitute the *reality* of things. Plants, animals and human beings came to be regarded as simply complex structures of atoms, and their behaviour was held as being explicable, ultimately, in terms of physical processes. From its beginnings in physics and astronomy, that way of seeing things came to dominate chemistry in the late eighteenth century, biology in the late nineteenth century, and the human sciences in the twentieth century. It is what ultimately lies behind the MEDICAL MODEL and the contemporary obsession with measurable outcomes, performance criteria and so on. Of course, there is a place for 'criteria', but what happens in practice is that the criteria become more important than what they were criteria *for.* For example, the results of personality tests are taken to constitute the *reality* of the person's personality. Similarly, the statistics of hospital waiting lists are taken to reveal the reality of reduced waiting times when, in fact, the waiting time has been 'reduced' by offering people 'holding sessions', in which case they are removed from the waiting list. Once the main emphasis is on the *criteria* one just needs to change the criteria in order to make it seem that the reality has changed.

The idea of a fully quantifiable reality is so embedded in our way of thinking that it is hard to see what alternatives there could be. Yet there *are* alternatives. We know this because there *have been* such alternatives in the past. Before the seventeenth century, the dominant way of seeing the world was that which originated from Aristotle. Aristotle and his successors didn't see the world as a giant MECHANISM but as an organic system full of potentials, meanings, tendencies, powers. Living things such as plants were fundamentally different from inorganic matter. Animals had all the life-characteristics of plants but in addition were sentient beings, and human beings had everything that animals had plus a capacity to reflect and reason. Aristotle was not just a philosopher, in the modern sense of that word, but a scientific thinker who developed sophisticated theories in physics, biology and psychology. From the point of view of twenty-first century science these theories seem quaint, wrong, not scientific at all, but that is a prejudiced way to see them (Lang, 1998). The ARISTOTELIANS had a science; it was just a very different kind of science from the one we are familiar with.

What happened following the developments in the seventeenth century was that the world was reduced to 'matter', although an exception had to be made in the case of human beings for 'consciousness' or 'mind'. Plants and animals were reduced entirely to being MECHANISMS. Later, some thinkers—and many philosophers still today—held that human beings also could be understood as complex MECHANISTIC systems and, conversely, that machines could be conscious. Recently, we have seen something of the absurdity of the situation in a government report on the rights of robots:

> Robots could one day demand the same citizen's rights as humans, according to a study by the British government. If granted, countries would be obliged to provide social benefits including housing and even 'robo-healthcare', the report says. The predictions are contained in nearly 250 papers that look ahead at developments over the next 50 years. (BBC news report, December 2006).

This *is* nonsense—isn't it? But it is something that clearly follows from the MECHANISTIC picture of the world.

Gendlin's theory explicitly opposes the MECHANISTIC picture. It draws on the work of many philosophers, not least Aristotle. Of course we cannot return to the ARISTOTELIAN way of seeing the world: too much of importance to us is grounded in what the MECHANISTIC MODEL has given us. Modern science and culture has gained much from that model, but it is important also to see what we have lost. In particular, we have lost our sense of there being life and SENTIENCE in the world; we have lost the sense of our continuity and community with nature, of the presence of purposiveness and meaning in the world, of the interconnectedness of things. Many of us are acutely aware of all this but we don't have an alternative way of thinking that can inform what we intuitively feel. What is needed is a radically different model, which is what Gendlin provides.

A second thinker on whom Gendlin draws is the eighteenth century philosopher Immanuel Kant. Kant's philosophy is difficult, but he is important for bringing out the point that human EXPERIENCING contains two distinct elements. There is the element of immediate feeling or sensation and the element of meaning or concepts. Both elements are always present to some extent but sometimes one is much more prominent than the other. For example, if we are blindfolded and given an object to touch we will be very aware of the sensations we have—that the object feels very soft at one end with a curious springy texture, while at the other end it is smooth and rounded. In this EXPERIENCING the sensations are prominent, although some concepts are there too— the concepts of 'soft', 'hard' etc. But we don't have any understanding of what the object is, not even of what general category it falls under: for instance, is it an artefact or some naturally occurring thing? We are aware of *it* through our sensations of it, through its feel, but we don't know *what* it is, what *kind* of thing it is. Experiences such as this draw our attention to the sensory–feeling element in our EXPERIENCING.

The opposite kind of case is where we are so involved in making conceptual distinctions that we are hardly aware of the immediate sensations involved. For example, think of someone who is identifying birds, using an illustrated bird book. They spot an oystercatcher, then a little tern—and that one over there—it's another oystercatcher. They don't pause to register anything of the 'feel' of the different birds, or any difference in feel between the two oystercatchers. Their EXPERIENCING runs mainly along a conceptual track, although of course they have to have various sensations in order for the bird-concepts to have something to apply to. Another example would be that of the tourist who sees the architecture in a new country entirely through the concepts that are presented in the tourist guide. They are tuned into those general concepts, rather than into the immediacy of their sensations, and do not really *see* the buildings in front of them.

In all our EXPERIENCING, the sensory–feeling element and the conceptual–understanding element are interwoven. If we just had general concepts they would be empty, abstract forms without application to our immediate feelings. And if we just had feelings we would have no idea what the feelings were—they would have no meaning. As Kant (1781/1933, A51/B75) put it, 'Without sensibility no object would be given to us, without understanding no object would be thought. Thoughts without content are empty; intuitions [this is Kant's terminology, but he means sensations or feelings] without concepts are blind.' In our actual lived EXPERIENCING there are both elements: the particular, immediate feeling–awareness in the here and now, an awareness of *this* and, at least to some extent, an understanding of *what* this is.

The interplay between concepts and feeling is something we can see in any focusing session—we have a problem that we can *feel* and which is formulated or conceptualised in a particular way. We give our attention to what we feel and now the formulation often changes. Focusing would be impossible without *both* elements in our EXPERIENCING and the *interaction* between the two.

The idea of an interaction between the two elements in our EXPERIENCING lies behind Piaget's ideas on the growth of understanding in the child, especially of 'ASSIMILATION' (the fitting of experiences into pre-existing COGNITIVE structures) and 'ACCOMMODATION' (the adapting of the structures to fit with new EXPERIENCING) (Hamlyn, 1967). Through Piaget this idea has come to inform the theory of PROCESS-EXPERIENTIAL THERAPY, where it is known as 'DIALECTICAL CONSTRUCTIVISM' (Greenberg et al., 1993). But it is there too in the background of focusing.

A third main source of Gendlin's thinking lies in the kind of philosophical approach known as 'PHENOMENOLOGY'. PHENOMENOLOGY explicitly rejects the 'scientific' view of the world as an account of the nature of reality. It starts with the *human* world, the world as it is *for us*. The human world is more basic than the conceptual framework of science. It is, after all, human beings who have created science. Science has been developed as *one* way of seeing things, a way that is especially useful if one wants to predict and control the course of events. Where we have other aims we need a *different* conceptual framework.

Fourthly, Gendlin draws significantly on the work of George H. Mead (Mead, 1934; Joas, 1985), best known as one of the founders of social psychology but also a philosopher of great originality. Mead was one of the earliest thinkers to suggest that, rather than starting with people as atomistic individuals, we should begin with personal *interaction*. For Mead, interaction is more basic than the individuals who are formed from the interactions, and Gendlin's 'process model' is built on this idea of 'INTERACTION FIRST'. Mead also adds something important to Aristotle's idea that animal life is built on plant life and human rational consciousness on animal SENTIENCE. He begins to show how we can get from animal behaviour to SYMBOLIC behaviour. There is a big gap here: think of the difference between raising your arm in order to reach something above you and raising it in order to vote. They are the same movement, perhaps even the same nerve firings, in a sense the same behaviour, but one is *just* behaviour while the other has *meaning*. The question is how we get from mere behaviour to meaning and Mead shows, at least in outline, how this is done.

Gendlin's philosophy can be seen to some extent as a CARRYING-FORWARD and elaboration of this work of Mead so as to show how the symbolic world can arise out of what is not symbolic. In this way he could be seen to be tracing the origins of Kant's distinction between felt experience and concepts. Felt experience belongs with the body and behaviour, concepts are a matter of meaning and SYMBOLISM. In human life the two are utterly intertwined and, where something goes wrong in the interaction between them, there we have a distinctively human problem.

Focusing works with the interaction between feeling and meaning. The focusing-oriented approach sees psychological disturbance as essentially a disturbance in that interaction. For instance, we get caught in our conceptual thinking, so that it is no longer informed by our feelings, or we are lost in our feelings and can't make adequate sense of them. To adapt Kant's remark above (p. 85), 'Concepts without felt experience are empty; felt experience without concepts is blind.'

Gendlin's theory is a radical rethinking of the conceptual scheme which we have inherited from the seventeenth century. It replaces 'things' with 'processes' and 'interactions', it restores the unity of the person as a living, SENTIENT, reflective being; it restores our community with the *other* living and sentient beings with whom we share our world. At the same time, it does not deny the possibility and value of thinking about people, for special purposes, *as if* they were machines. The surgeon, for example, may need to do that for the purposes of surgery. Gendlin does not reject or despise our technology, but a person *is not* a machine; a person is a living, SENTIENT, reflective being, utterly different in kind from a machine (Gendlin, 1997, Chapter 4a).

Counselling urgently needs a developed alternative model with which to counter the ill effects of the MECHANISTIC MODEL. Many people are working on such alternative ways of thinking and Gendlin's way will not be the only one with potential for the future of counselling. However, as a way of thinking that has developed, from the start, out of close attention to human EXPERIENCING and human difficulties, it is a theory that is likely to be especially relevant to the work of counsellors and psychotherapists.

12

RESEARCH INTO FOCUSING AND
FOCUSING-ORIENTED COUNSELLING

Outcome research

As counsellors, we tend to take it for granted that we are (fairly often) able to help (a significant number of) our clients. Concerning some clients we may conclude that we really did not help them at all, or not very much. It is often hard to know, and there are often large discrepancies between what clients and counsellors perceive as the helpful aspects of the sessions (Bohart & Tallman, 1999). The doubts that we may sometimes have about the effectiveness of counselling are, of course, magnified in our society as a whole. There are those who are totally sceptical about the effectiveness of counselling. There are also those who are sceptical about particular forms of counselling but not about others. For example, in the British National health Service (NHS) there is a perception that CBT is an effective form of counselling, whereas PERSON-CENTRED and PSYCHODYNAMIC approaches are less well valued. Given the demand and need for counselling and the limited resources of the NHS, it is inevitable that the questions should be raised of what evidence there is that counselling is effective and which approaches are more effective than the others.

Fortunately, there has grown up in the last twenty years or so a considerable body of evidence that counselling often is effective, that it is more effective than ordinary GP care and more effective than simply getting on with one's life. Pete Sanders (2006) summarises this work in the 'Person-Centred' volume of this series. It provides, I believe, an adequate answer to those who are sceptical about the effectiveness of counselling in general.

When it comes to the question of which approaches to counselling are the most effective, the research evidence is again clear, at least in connection with those approaches that have been researched (Bohart & Tallman, 1999). The major approaches—CBT, PERSON-CENTRED and PSYCHODYNAMIC are equally effective.

There are some studies that suggest differences, but these differences are nearly always correlated with the allegiance of the investigator. That is, CBT investigators tend to find that CBT is more effective and PROCESS-EXPERIENTIAL therapists find that PET is more effective. When these biases are allowed for, the original conclusion re-emerges: the different approaches are equally effective. This conclusion has become known in the research literature as the 'DODO-BIRD EFFECT'—a term deriving from the episode in *Alice in Wonderland* where the dodo says at the conclusion of a race, 'Everyone has won, and all must have prizes.'

The DODO-BIRD EFFECT is, for most counsellors, puzzling and disturbing. It is certainly something that requires an explanation. I think that from a focusing-oriented point of view it is possible to see something of what the explanation may be.

As I said at the start of this book, F-OC is best seen not as another school of therapy alongside CBT, PSYCHODYNAMIC and PERSON-CENTRED, but as a way of bringing into any form of counselling a particular orientation: an orientation towards the lived experiencing of the client and towards helping the client to SYMBOLISE and CARRY FORWARD their EXPERIENCING. From a focusing-oriented point of view, it is of relatively little importance whether a therapist reflects, makes interpretations, uses chair work, brings attention to the specifics of the client–therapist relationship, works with dreams, or any other procedure. Nor is it of much importance whether the counsellor grounds their interventions in one particular theory rather than another, such as learning theory, Rogers' theory of conditions of worth, Freudian theory, Lacanian theory and so on.

From a focusing-oriented perspective it is not the theories and procedures that matter, but how they are employed and how the client interacts with them. The crucial thing is whether a procedure is used in such a way that it helps the client to bring attention to their own EXPERIENCING so that they can SYMBOLISE and CARRY FORWARD that EXPERIENCING. The differences in the procedures and the theories don't matter too much. However, the main differences between the therapy schools just *are* differences in procedures and in theories. So, from a focusing-oriented point of view, it would be very *surprising* if one school of therapy were significantly more effective than any other. The focusing-oriented approach *entails* the DODO-BIRD EFFECT and so this phenomenon actually provides support for the approach.

The next research question is whether therapy (any therapy) *done in a focusing-oriented sort of way* is more effective than therapy done in other ways.

Much more work needs to be done in this area but there is already enough to be encouraging for focusing-oriented practitioners. First there are the studies of what the generally effective elements in counselling are. According to Orlinsky et al. (1994), what is important for outcome is not so much *what* clients talk about but *how they talk about it* (p. 296). Among the more specific variables favouring successful outcome are such things as the quality of the therapeutic relationship, client co-operation rather than resistance to therapy, and client openness rather than defensiveness. A further significant factor is 'client self-relatedness', which is a variable closely related to 'EXPERIENCING LEVEL'. These are all variables that one would expect to be important from the focusing-oriented perspective. The quality of the therapeutic relationship is crucial because it is this that creates the safety that is needed for the client to engage with their EXPERIENCING; client co-operation is crucial because in F-OC client and therapist work *together* at facilitating the client's SYMBOLISATION of their EXPERIENCING, and openness rather than defensiveness is clearly essential to any work with one's EXPERIENCING. Finally the importance of 'client self-relatedness' is a more specific confirmation of the principles of F-OC. In F-OC we help the client to engage with their own EXPERIENCING; what is important is not only the therapist's relationship with the client but the client's relationship with their 'inner client'. Thus, in this extensive research, there seems to be little that contradicts the principles of F-OC and much that is supportive of them.

In addition to this general research evidence, there are a number of studies which directly address the question of the effectiveness of focusing. Amongst these are the original studies undertaken by Gendlin and his associates using the EXPERIENCING

SCALE, which are discussed further in Purton (2004). A fuller review of the direct evidence in support of the effectiveness of focusing and of F-OC can be found in Hendricks (2002).

PROCESS RESEARCH

In addition to the outcome research discussed above, there is an increasing body of research into the detailed processes of focusing. The EXPERIENCING SCALE continues to be used and Iberg (2002) has developed scales for measuring the extent to which focusing has occurred in a session. These scales measure such things as the degree to which clients are 'friendly' towards their EXPERIENCING, to what extent a FELT SENSE forms, and to what extent there is 'release' or 'CARRYING-FORWARD'. With these scales it is possible to investigate such things as whether there is much correlation between therapist's and focuser's ratings on the scales (there is), and whether client satisfaction with a session is correlated with the level of focusing in the session (it is).

Other research (Clark, 1990) suggests that focusing may be helpful to unassertive clients because it gives them a better sense of what their EXPERIENCING *is*; that focusing-oriented therapists need to be careful not to emphasise the 'task' aspect of focusing to the detriment of the therapeutic bond, and that it is helpful for trainees to approach focusing work with clients through encouraging receptivity towards EXPERIENCING, rather than as a technique with specific steps.

Studies have also been done (Sachse, 1990a,1990b) on the effects of therapist response on the 'depth' of client EXPERIENCING. Sachse found that when therapists respond in a relatively 'shallow' way (e.g. judgementally, or purely INTELLECTUALLY), the subsequent client response tends to be shallower than previously. Conversely, if the therapist responds at a slightly deeper level than the client, the client's next response tends to be 'deeper'. Sachse found also that the therapists of the more successful clients tended to make more 'deepening' responses than the therapists of less successful clients.

PRACTITIONER RESEARCH

There is much scope for counsellors to engage in research into focusing and focusing-oriented counselling. Focusing sessions can easily be recorded and the moment-by-moment process can be studied. Recording sessions between focusing partners eliminates some of the difficulties inherent in recording client sessions.

Focusing lends itself to both QUALITATIVE and QUANTITATIVE approaches: for those interested in QUANTITATIVE methods many scales are available from the experiential researchers' website (see Appendix, p. 107). Amongst these are the EXPERIENCING SCALE and Iberg's scales discussed above. These instruments can be used very effectively for small-scale research, and the results of the research can be posted on the website without having to be prepared for formal publication.

QUALITATIVE RESEARCH opens up a whole range of possibilities. There are many questions that are currently unanswered about focusing. Here are some examples:

- Gendlin has often said that the FELT SENSE is normally experienced in the central part of the body, but some experienced focusing teachers report that there are focusers who experience FELT SENSES elsewhere in the body and even *outside* the body. How common is this? Does it make any difference to the focusing process?
- The FELT SENSE is described as a *BODY* SENSE. But some people query this emphasis on the body. Can you have a FELT SENSE of something but no specific awareness of it in the body?
- F-OC makes a rather sharp distinction between emotions and FELT SENSES, whereas in PROCESS-EXPERIENTIAL THERAPY the distinction is more blurry. Is this an important issue? Is it important for a focuser to be clear that what they have is a FELT SENSE rather than an emotion?
- Sometimes a FELT SENSE is CARRIED FORWARD by an image, sometimes by a word or phrase. Does it make much difference which mode of SYMBOLISATION the focuser uses? In an early paper, Gendlin (1970, p. 222) suggests that imagery and

verbal language work differently.

• It is possible to CARRY FORWARD a FELT SENSE in bodily movement, gesture or dance. Again, what differences are there in these modes of SYMBOLISATION? Are these more 'bodily' forms of CARRYING-FORWARD more effective for some people, or with some kinds of difficulties?

• Are there different modes of CARRYING-FORWARD, in the sense that, for example, one could CARRY FORWARD one's FELT SENSE of a painful situation by *writing a poem about it* rather than by finding a way of resolving the situation?

• Some focusing teachers strongly emphasise the form of words one uses in focusing, e.g. one is to say, 'I'm noticing that a part of me is scared', rather than 'I am scared'. How much difference do these linguistic distinctions make to the effectiveness of focusing?

• Focusing has something in common with meditative practices. What are the similarities and differences? Is it helpful to meditate before focusing or to focus before meditating?

• What is the effect of different body postures on focusing? Can focusing be done effectively while lying down or standing up? What difference does it make if your eyes are open or closed?

• What are the effects of different styles of accompanying the focuser? Mountford (2006) has suggested that there is a continuum from a very active, engaged, eyes-open style of focusing to a receptive, meditative, eyes-closed style. Are different styles preferable for some people, or with particular kinds of difficulty?

• What difference does it make if you focus alone or with a partner? Are there advantages and disadvantages of each way?

• Can you be supported in your EXPERIENCING through interaction with the natural world rather than with a human being? Is it true that, just as the body can in a sense 'talk back', so can a tree or a river? Murphy (2006) has studied such experiences in connection with ecopsychology.

This list could go on for much longer! Perhaps it will encourage you to reflect on what catches your interest in focusing and to consider ways in which you might carry that interest forward.

13

FOCUSING-ORIENTED COUNSELLING
AND THE SCHOOLS OF THERAPY

In this final chapter I want to say a bit more about the relationship of F-OC to the various 'schools' of counselling and psychotherapy. These comments will be brief: if you are especially interested in a particular school of counselling you may want to look further at how its ideas and methods could be enriched or challenged by the principles of F-OC. Very little work has been done in this area— there is plenty of space for carrying it forward!

F-OC has rather special and specific connections with PERSON-CENTRED THERAPY, PROCESS-EXPERIENTIAL THERAPY and INTEGRATIVE THERAPY. I will come to these. With regard to the other schools, the issues that arise are more straightforward and are of two sorts: one to do with the procedures and one to do with the concepts of the particular schools. In such a brief discussion there is always the danger of caricaturing the procedures and concepts involved, but I will have to take that risk!

GESTALT THERAPY

Regarding procedures, we have already seen how F-OC can employ the GESTALT THERAPY two-chair procedure. The difference between the GESTALT and the focusing-oriented employment of the procedure is that when used in a focusing-oriented way the procedure is not automatically proposed just because the client has a particular sort of problem; it is always introduced tentatively; it takes up only a part of the session; it is dropped if the client doesn't find it helpful; and time is taken afterwards to follow through the changes in the client's EXPERIENCING which result from the procedure. Of course, some GESTALT therapists may themselves work like this, and then the differences between the F-O and the GESTALT version of the session may become insignificant. Much the same applies to the use of other GESTALT 'experiments'.

PSYCHODYNAMIC THERAPY

PSYCHODYNAMIC counsellors work with INTERPRETATIONS. A client talks about their relationship with their partner and the therapist suggests that this feels similar to their relationship to their mother. An INTERPRETATIVE link is made that does not come from the client. INTERPRETATIONS are not ruled out in F-OC but the spirit in which they are made is different from the PSYCHODYNAMIC spirit. The latter involves the idea that there are general patterns in human development and personality that are known to the therapist but not to the client. Because of their greater knowledge, the therapist can know better than the client what is going on in the client. They can then draw the client's attention to things of which the client is UNCONSCIOUS, and the client acquires 'insight' or is seen as resisting such insight.

From a focusing-oriented point of view the therapist *doesn't* know what is going on in the client. Strictly speaking, in focusing theory it is not even determinate what *is* going on in the client until the client expresses it. On the other hand the focusing-oriented counsellor may be familiar with some PSYCHODYNAMIC concepts and may sense that such concepts might be helpful to this client. Or the *client* might be interested in PSYCHODYNAMIC ideas and, with such a client, the focusing-oriented counsellor might try out the notion that, for example, the client's difficulty in asserting himself with his partner is connected to what he has said about his mother. One client might find the notion of the OEDIPUS COMPLEX really helpful here, another might resonate with the Jungian notion of the Terrible Mother ARCHETYPE.

The question in F-OC is not whether the PSYCHODYNAMIC INTERPRETATIONS are 'true representations of what is going on in the client' but whether they have an experiential impact on the client. The client's own EXPERIENCING and formulation of their EXPERIENCING are primary. On the other hand the therapist's concepts may stimulate new EXPERIENCING in the client and the formation of a new FELT SENSE of the client's situation. When the situation has been formulated along the lines of a particular theory it may no longer feel quite the same. The client now notices things that they had not felt before (for example, 'there *is* something here to do with my mother … ') and that change is real whether or not they believe in the theory that has led to it. The focusing-oriented way with an INTERPRETATION is to try it *if* the counsellor has a FELT SENSE that the INTERPRETATION might help, to drop it immediately if it does not RESONATE with the client, to check what the client's EXPERIENCING is following the INTERPRETATION, and not to *fill* the session with INTERPRETATIONS.

BEHAVIOURAL THERAPY

Much the same applies to the procedures of all the schools. BEHAVIOURAL therapists work with DESENSITISATION techniques. If someone wants to be able to go into pubs on their own but is too scared to do so the behaviour therapist may, with the client, work out a scheme of small DESENSITISING steps—the first time, just go down the street and then come home. The next time go to the pub door but don't go in. When that becomes comfortable, go to the door, look in, and come away. Then go in with someone else and let them leave a minute before you do. This can work. The behaviourist theory is that it works by conditioning, by the same sort of process as that involved in taming or training animals. They say you should give yourself a treat with each successful small step.

It can work, but one thing that can go wrong with behavioural programmes is that they can lose touch with the client's EXPERIENCING. Therapist and client negotiate at the start what goals are to be achieved, but from then on it is just technique, as it would be with training an animal. However, a person's goals may *change* as a result of their experience. Having looked into the pub the client may feel they really don't think much of pub life at all. Each step in the behavioural programme needs to be checked back with the experience of it. 'How did that feel? Do I want to continue with this, do I want to continue with this in this way? I'm not sure … let's look at what it feels like now … Hmmm … .' And while an animal needs to be rewarded by the trainer for achieving each step in the programme, a person needs rather to register—to really feel—the satisfaction of each step achieved. This is its own reward; it comes from within, from the client, and is not something externally managed. What F-OC brings to the behavioural approach is the constant reference back to the FELT SENSE of what is happening.

COGNITIVE THERAPY

COGNITIVE therapists have a procedure of challenging negative thoughts or REFRAMING how the client thinks about their situation. For instance, a student is terrified of giving a presentation in class. The therapist says (Beck, 1976, p. 251) '… you tend to regard any failure as though it's the end of the world … . What you have to do is to get your failures labelled correctly—as failure to reach a goal, not as disaster. You have to start to challenge your wrong premises.' This may help (as it seems to with the client whom Beck is discussing), and then it seems that COGNITIVE REFRAMING is a really deep and powerful technique. The COGNITIVE theory is that it works because changing the thoughts changes the feelings, and changing the feelings changes the behaviour. But of course it does not *always* work—the client may respond by saying, 'What you say is of course true but it makes no difference to how I feel', and then the COGNITIVE approach looks rather shallow and ineffective. From a focusing-oriented point of view the crucial thing is whether the COGNITIVE REFRAMING has an experiential impact. A helpful piece of REFRAMING carries forward what was already IMPLICIT in the client and then it looks as if the change comes simply from the new thinking. Yet with the next client the same piece of REFRAMING may have no impact at all. It is clearly not the case that we can effectively REFRAME our situations in any way we choose. If that were so life would be very simple! What is needed is a not *a* REFRAMING, or a *rational* REFRAMING, but a REFRAMING that carries forward the client's EXPERIENCING.

PROCEDURES AND CONCEPTS

Most of what I have just said is about bringing the *procedures* of the different therapy schools into F-OC—for example chair work, INTERPRETATION, DESENSITISING, COGNITIVE REFRAMING. Apart from INTERPRETATION, these procedures do not bring in much of the conceptual framework of the school in question. One can use DESENSITISATION without knowing or caring much about conditioning theory, or chair work without knowing much about GESTALT PSYCHOLOGY. PSYCHODYNAMIC INTERPRETATIONS are different—the interpretations are based on particular theories (Freudian, Jungian, Kleinian, etc.). You can't make Freudian INTERPRETATIONS without knowing the Freudian concepts. But can the Freudian concepts be brought into F-OC? Only in the way I have indicated above—as *possible* ways for the client to CARRY FORWARD their EXPERIENCING and not as descriptions of what is going on in the client. The concepts which are valuable for the client have to be concepts which RESONATE for *them*, which enliven rather than shut down their EXPERIENCING. It doesn't much matter where the concepts come from; the important question is whether they help the client.

PERSON-CENTRED THERAPY

The relationship between F-OC and PERSON-CENTRED THERAPY is a special one. Gendlin was strongly influenced by Rogers' work, and Rogers was influenced by Gendlin (Purton, 2004). F-OC is regarded by the World Association for Person-Centered and Experiential Psychotherapy and Counselling (WAPCEPC) as an important member of the PERSON-CENTRED 'family'. Or, in Margaret Warner's metaphor, it can be seen as one of the 'tribes of the person-centred nation' (Warner, 2000; Sanders, 2004). Within the PERSON-CENTRED nation, F-OC needs to be distinguished from the other 'tribes'. I will discuss its relationship to PROCESS-EXPERIENTIAL THERAPY below and here say a little about how it stands in relation to two other forms of PERSON-CENTRED COUNSELLING.

One form derives mainly from Rogers' early approach, which Barrett-Lennard (1998) has characterised as 'non-directive reflective therapy'. This approach emphasises empathy and mainly uses REFLECTION as a vehicle for empathy. The REFLECTIVE procedure in this form of PERSON-CENTRED COUNSELLING is little different from that in F-OC, although, as we have seen, in F-OC the reasons for REFLECTING go beyond the embodiment of empathy.

The other form of PERSON-CENTRED COUNSELLING derives more from Rogers' later emphasis on congruence and on relationship. It sees the therapeutic situation as one in which the therapist as a whole, authentic person provides a healing presence for the client simply by being with the client in an accepting and empathic way. No techniques are employed and the therapist has no goals in mind. It is a therapy of 'being' rather than of 'doing'. Training in this approach emphasises personal development, since becoming an effective therapist is held to be not a matter of developing skills but of becoming an authentic person. This approach is radically different from any other form of therapy. In it the therapist as a whole person meets the client as a whole person. F-OC also has this emphasis on the *whole*, but differs in that it constantly moves between the whole and *facets* of the whole. Most forms of therapy emphasise one or other facet of the person, such as COGNITION, imagery or emotion and can miss the whole person. The kind of PERSON-CENTRED THERAPY that we are considering here emphasises, by contrast, the whole person, but tends to miss the importance of working with particular aspects. If most therapeutic schools tend to miss the wood for the trees, this form of PERSON-CENTRED THERAPY seems to me to miss the trees for the wood. The issues here constitute lively tensions in the PERSON-CENTRED movement!

PROCESS-EXPERIENTIAL THERAPY

PROCESS-EXPERIENTIAL THERAPY—alternatively known as 'EMOTION-FOCUSED THERAPY'—(Greenberg et al., 1993; Elliott et al., 2004) also has a special relationship to F-OC. It is another of the 'tribes of the PERSON-CENTRED nation'. PET values focusing but sees it as one procedure or 'task' amongst others, which include active listening, evocative responding and several kinds of chair work. The underlying idea of PET is that psychological troubles are due to dysfunctional EMOTION SCHEMES in the client. There are various ways in which emotional processing can be dysfunctional, and for each of these 'process difficulties' a particular therapeutic procedure is prescribed. Focusing is prescribed for situations in which the client has an unclear FELT SENSE of their problem. The details of the relationship between F-OC and PET are something on which much more work needs to be done. Certainly F-OC can benefit from the careful analysis of process difficulties which is still being carried out by PET theorists. The differences between F-OC and PET may lie mainly in the background philosophies, and in the emphasis which PET places on emotion, in contrast to the emphasis which F-OC places on the FELT SENSE.

INTEGRATIVE THERAPY

We come finally to the special case of INTEGRATIVE THERAPY. Richard Worsley (2004) has drawn attention to two different senses of 'integration' in counselling. One is where the therapist integrates different procedures into their work. F-OC provides a framework within which this can be done. The basic principle is that although in F-OC we work with the whole person, and with the FELT SENSE of the whole situation, what leads up to and flows from the felt sense may be much more specific. For instance, the client may begin with particular thoughts or emotions that are involved in their difficulty, and from these move to a FELT SENSE of the whole thing. Then, staying with the FELT SENSE, something new comes. It might be an image, or a formulation of a dilemma. From here, the client can be helped to work with the image or with the dilemma. The therapist will be more helpful to the client if they know something about how one might work with images (for instance Jungian 'amplification') or dilemmas (for instance two-chair work). Then the session returns to the FELT SENSE. How does the whole thing feel now? What might the next step be? The *FELT SENSE* is the link between the different modes of approach (thought, feeling, imagery, etc.) and between the different therapeutic procedures. The FELT SENSE is the sense of the whole, deeper than any of its specific manifestations.

Worsley's second sense of 'integration' is that of the

integration of *theories. Can* the different theories be integrated? To a very limited extent this seems possible. CBT brings together some of the ideas of COGNITIVE and of BEHAVIOURAL THERAPY, and in a similar way COGNITIVE-ANALYTICAL THERAPY (CAT) brings together, to some extent, PSYCHODYNAMIC concepts with COGNITIVE theory. The difficulty with theory integration is that the theories use *different* concepts. The concepts don't mesh with each other, especially if we are thinking of schemes as different as behaviouristic learning theory and the Freudian notion of the UNCONSCIOUS. Either the conceptual schemes contradict each other or they simply bypass one another. The bringing together of different theories will involve theoretical *change.* They can't be integrated *as they are.*

It is conceivable that one day an overall counselling theory will be developed that is so successful that it will eliminate all its rivals while perhaps incorporating certain aspects of the 'old' theories. In Kuhn's (1962/1996) scheme of the history of science this would amount to the coming of counselling's first real 'PARADIGM'. But that may be just a fantasy. It seems equally likely that the different theories will continue to be developed and that the idea of multiple theories will become more acceptable. The POSTMODERNIST view is that there are many ways of seeing the world, none of which is *the* truth. There can be many truths. However, Gendlin's approach has something important to add to POSTMODERNISM. It is the idea that there really is a world out there, independent of our theories. The world is *that which is formulated in different ways by the different theories.* The world is much *more* than can be formulated by our theories, but when we approach it with a particular theory it responds in a particular way. Our theories can draw out different aspects of the world. So far as counselling is concerned this means that there may be times in a counselling session when Freud's theory pulls out something that would not be pulled out by ideas of conditioning and reinforcement. This does not mean that the ultimate truth is that the client has an unresolved OEDIPUS COMPLEX, but that there is *something* there which can for the moment be formulated in that way. Later, the client might formulate *it* in a different way. The important thing is that there *is* an 'it'—'it' can be felt, it is part of the client's EXPERIENCING, but there may be many ways of SYMBOLISING 'it' and CARRYING 'it' FORWARD. (We discover that when we become familiar with focusing.)

We may rightly feel that 'there is only one world out there' but this need not mean that we should aim at the construction of a unified *theory*. There are advantages in having many theories because each of them draws attention to different facets of the world. It may be as well if the different schools of therapy maintain their identities—one can belong to a particular school and develop new aspects of its way of working without needing to think that the other schools are 'wrong'. In any case, the schools of therapy do not really embody neat, coherent bodies of theory and practice. The procedures are not necessarily well-grounded in the respective theories and the procedures of the different schools overlap. (Kohutians as well as Rogerians use REFLECTION, Gestalt therapists as well as Jungians work with dreams.) The unity of a school of therapy is not so much a unity of theory or practice but an institutional unity grounded in shared reading, training programmes, professional organisations, networks of SUPERVISION etc. (Gendlin, 1996, pp. 169, 172). A counsellor belonging to the 'X' school may find that, in practice, they have more in common with *some* counsellors belonging to the 'Y' school than with *some* counsellors belonging to their own school.

So far as theory is concerned, rather than thinking in terms of a 'super-theory', which—impossibly—would combine all the current theories, the way ahead is more likely to be via a 'META-THEORY', that is, a theory about theories. Gendlin's theory is of this sort. (Quite different META-THEORIES are IMPLICIT in POSTMODERNISM and in more traditional accounts of scientific theory development, such as that of Popper (1959).) Gendlin's META-THEORY shows how there can be different theories, while allowing for the idea that there is a world out there which is independent of the theories. There is far more to the world (and our situations and our EXPERIENCING) than can be 'caught' in our theories, yet the theories do catch *something*. We bring our theories up to our EXPERIENCING and the interaction between them elicits new experiences that we would not have had without those theories. Seen in this way the theory and practice of F-OC provide the foundation for a truly INTEGRATIVE model of counselling, which nevertheless allows for the continued existence of the different schools.

APPENDIX
RESOURCES FOR LEARNING

ORGANISATIONS

The Focusing Institute
   34 East Lane, Spring Valley, NY 10977, USA
   Tel. 845 362 5222, Fax. 845 678 2276
   email: info@focusing.org website: <www.focusing.org>
International Association of Focusing-Oriented Therapies.
   <www.focusingtherapy.org>
British Focusing Teachers Association (BFTA)
   '... an association of people in Britain who are teaching or using Focusing in a professional context. BFTA exists to support the teaching of
   Focusing, the training of Focusing practitioners ... the further development of Focusing professionals, other applications of Focusing (e.g.
   counselling and therapy), and the development of Focusing groups.'
   <www.focusing.org.uk>
*World Association for Person-Centered and Experiential
Psychotherapy and Counseling (WAPCEPC).*
   <www.pce-world.org>
Focusing Resources
   2625 Alcatraz Ave, PMB #202, Berkeley, CA 94705 USA.
   Tel. 1 510 666 9948.
   email: <awcornell@pacbell.net> <www.focusingresources.com>

JOURNALS

The Focusing Folio. Journal of the Focusing Institute.
The Focusing Connection. Published by Focusing Resources.
Person-Centered and Experiential Psychotherapies. The quarterly
   journal of WAPCEPC.

WEBSITES

Focusing Institute (New York) <www.focusing.org>
British Focusing Teachers Association (BFTA)
   <www.focusing.org.uk>
Centre for Counselling Studies, University of East Anglia
   <www.uea.ac.uk/edu/counsell.html>

Focusing Resources (Ann Weiser Cornell, USA)
   <www.focusingresources.com>
Peter Afford (London) <www.focusing.co.uk>
Rob Foxcroft (Glasgow) <www.robfoxcroft.com>
Barbara McGavin (Bath) <www.innerrelationship.com>
Campbell Purton (Norwich) <www.dwelling.me.uk>
Gendlin Online Library (GOL)

From late 2007 this will make available the work of Eugene Gendlin much of which has up to now been available only in difficult-to-find journals. The GOL will be hosted on the websites of the Focusing Institute and of the Centre for Counselling Studies at the University of East Anglia <www.uea.ac.uk/edu/counsell.html>.

FURTHER READING

Focusing: generally and as a self-help procedure

Gendlin, ET (2003) *Focusing*. London: Rider.

Cornell, AW (1996) *The Power of Focusing*. Oakland, CA: New Harbinger.

Cornell, AW (2005) *The Radical Acceptance of Everything*. Berkeley CA: Calluna Press.

Cornell, AW & McGavin, B (2002) *The Focusing Student's and Companion's Manual*. Berkeley CA: Calluna Press.

Friedman, N (2000) *Focusing: Selected Essays 1974–1999*. Xlibris Publishing: <www.Xlibris.com>.

Focusing-oriented counselling/psychotherapy

Gendlin, ET (1996) *Focusing-Oriented Psychotherapy*. New York: Guilford Press.

Purton, C (2004) Focusing-Oriented therapy. In P. Sanders (ed) *The Tribes of the Person-Centred Nation*. Ross-on-Wye: PCCS Books, pp. 45–65.

Purton, C (2004) *Person-Centred Therapy: The Focusing-Oriented Approach*. Basingstoke: Palgrave Macmillan.

Friedman, N. (2007) *Focusing-Oriented Therapy*. iUniverse: <www.iUniverse.com>.

Focusing theory

Gendlin, ET (1984) The client's client: The edge of awareness. In RL Levant & JM Shlien (eds) *Client-Centered Therapy and the*

Person-Centered Approach. New York: Praeger, pp. 76–107. See the second part of this chapter.

Gendlin, ET (1986) *Let Your Body Interpret Your Dreams.* Wilmette: Chiron. See Appendix A.

Gendlin, ET (1991) Thinking beyond patterns. In B den Ouden and M Moen (eds) *The Presence of Feeling in Thought.* New York: Peter Lang, pp. 21–151. Also available as a monograph from the Focusing Institute, New York.

Gendlin, ET (1997) *Experiencing and the Creation of Meaning.* Evanston, IL: Northwestern University Press.

Gendlin, ET (1997) *A Process Model.* New York: Focusing Institute.

Purton, C (2002) Focusing on focusing. In *Client-Centered and Experiential Psychotherapy in the 21st Century: Advances in Theory, Research and Practice.* Ross-on-Wye: PCCS Books, pp. 89–98.

Purton, C (2000–2004) A brief guide to A Process Model. *The Folio: A Journal For Focusing and Experiential Therapy*, pp. 112–120. (Also available at <www.dwelling.me.uk>).

DIPLOMA/M.A. PROGRAMME

Centre for Counselling Studies, University of East Anglia: Postgraduate Diploma/MA in Focusing and Experiential Psychotherapy. Full details on the UEA School of Education website: <www.uea.ac.uk/edu> (Look under 'Research and taught degrees'.) Or contact: Centre for Counselling Studies, University Counselling Service, University of East Anglia, Norwich NR4 7TJ. Tel: 01603 592656; email: <j.ramsbottom@uea.ac.uk>.

RESEARCH

Network for Research on Experiential Psychotherapies
  <www.experiential-researchers.org>

Research on focusing is detailed in Marion Hendricks 'Focusing-oriented/experiential psychotherapy' in DJ Cain & J Seeman (eds) (2002) *Humanistic Psychotherapies: Handbook of Research and Practice.* Washington: American Psychological Association, pp. 221–51.

GLOSSARY

(...) *see* ELLIPSIS

ACCOMMODATION (Piaget)   The process by which COGNITIVE structures are adapted to fit with new experiencing.

ACTION STEP   An action which the client takes in their life as a result of a FELT SHIFT that has come in focusing.

ACTUALISING TENDENCY (Rogers)   The tendency of organisms to achieve, maintain and enhance their potentials (see also LIFE-FORWARD).

ANALYTICAL THERAPY   Therapy based on the principles and procedures of the PSYCHODYNAMIC schools.

ARCHETYPE (Jung)   A universal human pattern manifested in characteristic images or behaviour. For example, the 'shadow', the 'earth mother', the '*PUER AETERNUS*'.

ARISTOTELIAN PHILOSOPHY   The philosophy of Aristotle (4th century BCE) which became the dominant philosophy during the Middle Ages in Europe. There is a strong ARISTOTELIAN background to Gendlin's thinking.

ASSIMILATION (Piaget)   The process of fitting experiences into pre-existing COGNITIVE structures.

BEHAVIOURAL THERAPY   Therapy based on the principles of behaviour theory, such as conditioning and reinforcement.

BODY SENSE   The feel of situations or problems in the body.

CARRYING-FORWARD   The movement from what is IMPLICIT to what is more EXPLICIT.

CATHARSIS   The release of emotion—originally an ARISTOTELIAN term meaning the purging of emotion in drama.

CLIENT'S CLIENT   The FELT SENSE, or EDGE OF AWARENESS, thought of as if it were the client's own inner client.

COGNITIVE   Relating to COGNITION or thought.

COGNITIVE ANALYTICAL THERAPY (CAT)   A form of therapy that combines ideas from COGNITIVE THERAPY and ANALYTICAL THERAPY.

COGNITIVE BEHAVIOURAL THERAPY (CBT)   A form of therapy that combines ideas from COGNITIVE THERAPY and BEHAVIOURAL THERAPY.

COGNITIVE REFRAMING   The re-conceptualisation of a problem or situation.

COGNITIVE THERAPY   A form of therapy that emphasises the importance of thinking and COGNITION in the generation and resolution of psychological problems.

CONSTRUALS   Ways of formulating problems or situations. The same events can be construed in many different ways.

CORE CONDITIONS (Rogers)   The three best-known of the six conditions that Rogers hypothesised to be necessary and sufficient for therapeutic change: empathy, unconditional positive regard, and authenticity.

DESENSITISATION   The BEHAVIOUR THERAPY procedure of helping a client to become less sensitive to troubling situations. Usually it involves gradually increasing the person's ability to tolerate the situation.

DIALECTICAL CONSTRUCTIVISM A view of the development of human knowledge deriving from the work of Jean Piaget as developed by Juan Pascual-Leone. Central to the theory of PROCESS-EXPERIENTIAL THERAPY, and has important affinities with Gendlin's theory of focusing.

DODO-BIRD EFFECT The research conclusion that all schools of counselling or psychotherapy have roughly the same degree of effectiveness. The phrase comes from a scene in Lewis Carroll's *Alice in Wonderland* where the Dodo says of a race 'Everyone has won and all must have prizes'.

EDGE OF AWARENESS Awareness that has not (yet) been formulated or conceptualised. The FELT SENSE is at the edge of awareness.

EGO STRENGTH PSYCHOANALYTIC concept referring to the strength and cohesion of a person's sense of self.

ELLIPSIS (...) Gendlin's device—often referred to as the 'dot-dot-dot'—for indicating something IMPLICIT, something not yet formulated in SYMBOLS.

EMOTION-FOCUSED THERAPY See PROCESS-EXPERIENTIAL THERAPY.

EMOTION SCHEME (PROCESS-EXPERIENTIAL THERAPY) A theoretical concept of a structure underlying and organising emotion, thought and perception.

EMOTIONAL OVERWHELM The state of being overwhelmed by or 'caught in' emotion.

EXISTENTIALISM A movement in philosophy deriving largely from the work of Kierkegaard, Heidegger and Sartre, which emphasises the unique existence of the individual, rather than thinking of human experience and behaviour in terma of general concepts and universal laws.

EXPERIENCING Our immediate felt awareness of our situation, containing elements of SENTIENCE and of understanding.

EXPERIENCING LEVEL A measure of the degree to which a client engages with their EXPERIENCING.

EXPERIENCING SCALE A scale developed by Gendlin and his colleagues to measure EXPERIENCING LEVEL. Very similar to Rogers' 'Process Scale'.

EXPLICIT Those aspects of our EXPERIENCING which have been formulated, conceptualised, put into words or other symbols. The opposite of IMPLICIT.

EXTERNALISING Talking in counselling about external events without expressing anything of one's own response to, or feelings about, the events.

FELT SENSE The 'feel' or 'sense' of a situation or problem *as a whole.*

FELT SHIFT The change in a FELT SENSE as one gives one's attention to it.

GESTALT PSYCHOLOGY A school of psychology which emphasises the holistic principles and self-organising tendencies of human beings.

GESTALT THERAPY A form of therapy developed by Fritz Perls and deriving from GESTALT PSYCHOLOGY, PSYCHOANALYSIS and EXISTENTIALISM. It makes much use of therapeutic procedures such as two-chair work and empty-chair work.

HANDLE WORDS Words (or other symbols) that allow the focuser to 'get a grip' on a felt sense so that if it is lost it can be recovered.

HUMANISTIC COUNSELLING   Covers the broad range of counselling schools that are not PSYCHODYNAMIC, COGNITIVE or BEHAVIOURAL; especially PERSON-CENTRED THERAPY, GESTALT THERAPY and EXISTENTIAL THERAPY.

IMPLICIT   That which is 'in the background' of our EXPERIENCING: what hasn't (yet) been fully formulated or conceptualised. The opposite of EXPLICIT.

INNER CRITIC   An element in the personality that rigidly and unreasonably criticises or condemns what we feel or do. To be distinguished from 'conscience'.

INTEGRATIVE COUNSELLING   Counselling that integrates the ideas and/or procedures of various counselling schools.

INTELLECTUALISING   Talking about one's problems in a COGNITIVE way that avoids any expression of feeling.

INTERACTION FIRST   Gendlin's term for the principle that individual things (experiences, people) are secondary to the interactive processes that give rise to them.

INTERPRETATION   A counsellor's formulation or conceptualisation of a client's EXPERIENCING with which the client may or may not agree.

INTERVENTION   Strictly speaking it means 'interference' (to stop something: to intervene). Often used to mean counsellor-response. Not frequently used in person-centred circles, some practitioners preferring to use 'contribution'.

LIFE-FORWARD   Gendlin's term for the sensed 'direction' of therapeutic change, also referred to as 'the direction of fresh air'.

LOGICAL THOUGHT   Moving by logical deduction from one thought to another without dipping down into the experiencing from which the thoughts come.

MECHANISTIC MODEL   The model of the world developed in the 17th century in which everything is thought about in terms of mechanisms, measurement and quantifiable experience.

MEDICAL MODEL   The view of counselling or psychotherapy which sees it as analogous to medical treatment. The medical model is grounded in the more general MECHANISTIC MODEL.

META-THEORY   A theory which is concerned with theories rather than with what the theories are about. Counselling theories are about the nature of counselling and therapeutic change; a meta-theory of counselling is about theories of counselling. Examples of meta-theories would be the POSTMODERNIST theory, in which there can be an indefinite number of theories in any field, none of which are more true than others, and Gendlin's theory, discussed briefly in Chapter 11 of this book.

MOMENT OF MOVEMENT   Rogers' term for what Gendlin calls a FELT SHIFT.

OEDIPUS COMPLEX/CONFLICT (Freud)   The PSYCHOANALYTIC concept according to which the young boy's attachment to his mother and hatred of his father needs to be 'worked through' so that it does not interfere with later relationships.

ORGANIC CONDITION/DISEASE   A condition or illness with a physical/biological cause (rather than psychological), e.g. brain tumours are physical (organic) entities but symptoms can in some circumstances look like the symptoms of psychological distress (mood swings). Also, e.g. delirium (hallucinations and delusions) caused by fever.

ORGANISMIC VALUING PROCESS (Rogers)   The process of EXPERIENCING and SYMBOLISING what is valued by the human organism.

PARADIGM (Kuhn)   In the history of science, the developed and agreed way of thinking about an area of science. Before the development of a paradigm there are many competing theories in that area of science. Then one theory predominates and the other ways of thinking are abandoned. For example, chemistry before the development of the atomic theory and—arguably—psychology today.

PERSON-CENTRED COUNSELLING/THERAPY   The school of therapy initiated by Carl Rogers and now incorporating classical client-centred therapy, focusing-oriented therapy and PROCESS-EXPERIENTIAL THERAPY.

PHENOMENOLOGY   Two related senses, both deriving from the work of Edmund Husserl. In one sense (the psychological sense) the approach to the study of psychology through the examination of subjective experiences. In another sense (the philosophical sense), the study of the objective forms or 'essences' of human experience without incorporating any theoretical assumptions.

POINTING   In focusing, the attempt to indicate what lies beyond the EXPLICIT. Words such as 'something' or 'that thing' are useful in pointing.

POSTMODERNISM   A diverse movement in late 20th century philosophy and culture characterised especially by the idea that there is no ultimate Truth or Reality, and that human beings construct, rather than discover, meanings and values.

PRIMARY PREVENTION RESEARCH   Looking at the factors which predispose people to certain conditions/distress, such as social and environmental conditions, and personal characteristics and experiences.

PROCESS-EXPERIENTIAL THERAPY   One of the sub-schools of PERSON-CENTRED THERAPY also known as EMOTION-FOCUSED THERAPY. It emphasises the theoretical notion of EMOTION SCHEMES and of particular therapeutic tasks that become appropriate when the client encounters particular difficulties in experiential process.

PSYCHODYNAMIC COUNSELLING   A school of counselling based on the ideas and procedures of psychoanalysis.

PUER AETERNUS (Jung)   An ARCHETYPE underlying the behaviour of men who 'do not grow up'.

QUALITATIVE RESEARCH   Research that uses non-quantitative methods of enquiry: concerned with the *qualities* of human experience and behaviour.

QUANTITATIVE RESEARCH   Research involving quantifiable data and often statistical analysis.

REFLECTION The 'saying back' of what a client has said. It can convey empathic understanding or help the client to go more deeply into their EXPERIENCING.

RESONATING In focusing, the 'checking' of whether what has been said CARRIES the focuser's EXPERIENCING FORWARD.

SENSITISE/SENSITISATION In focusing theory, the effect that theoretical knowledge can have in making the counsellor more sensitive to what the client *might* be EXPERIENCING.

SENTIENCE The sensory/feeling aspect of our EXPERIENCING, as contrasted with our conceptual understanding.

STEPS, EXPERIENTIAL The small movements in the therapeutic process. Contrasts with logical steps that do not come directly from EXPERIENCING. See also FELT SHIFT.

STRUCTURE-BOUND Gendlin's term for EXPERIENCING that has become fixed, 'frozen', inaccessible to change.

SYMBOLISATION The expression of EXPERIENCING in symbols such as words, images or gestures.

UNCONSCIOUS, THE Psychoanalytic concept of aspects of experience of which we are unaware. Focusing theory prefers the concept of that which is IMPLICIT.

UNFINISHED BUSINESS GESTALT concept applying to EXPERIENCING that has not been completed, especially in situations where an emotion has been suppressed.

REFERENCES

Barrett-Lennard, GT (1998) *Carl Rogers' Helping System: Journey and substance.* London: Sage.

BBC news report December 2006. <http://news.bbc.co.uk/1/hi/technology/6200005.stm> (Accessed 21 June 2007).

Beck, A (1976) *Cognitive Therapy and the Emotional Disorders.* London: Penguin.

Bennett, MR & Hacker, PMS (2003) *Philosophical Foundations of Neuroscience.* Oxford: Blackwell.

Bohart, AC & Tallman, K (1999) *How Clients Make Therapy Work.* Washington: American Psychological Association.

Clark, CA (1990) A comprehensive process analysis of focusing events in experiential therapy. Doctoral dissertation, University of Toledo.

Cornell, AW (1996) *The Power of Focusing.* Oakland CA: New Harbinger.

Cornell, AW (2005) *The Radical Acceptance of Everything.* Berkeley: Calluna Press.

Cornell, AW & McGavin, B (2002) *The Focusing Student's and Companion's Manual.* Berkeley CA: Calluna Press.

Davies, E & Burdett, J (2004) Preventing 'schizophrenia': Creating the conditions for saner societies. In J Read, LR Mosher & RP Bentall (eds) *Models of Madness: Psychological, social and biological approaches to schizophrenia.* London: Routledge, pp. 271–82.

Dijksterhuis, EJ (1961) *The Mechanization of the World Picture.* Oxford: Clarendon Press.

Durak, GM, Bernstein, R & Gendlin, ET (1997) Effects of focusing training on therapy process and outcome. *The Folio: A Journal for Focusing and Experiential Therapy, 15*, 2, 7–14.

Elliott, R, Watson, JC, Goldman, RN & Greenberg, LS (2004) *Emotion-Focused Therapy: Coaching clients to work through their feelings.* Washington DC: American Psychological Association.

Gendlin, ET (1962/1997) *Experiencing and the Creation of Meaning.* (2nd edn): Evanston, IL: Northwestern University Press (1997).

Gendlin, ET (1964/1973) A theory of personality change. In AR Mahrer and L Pearson (eds) *Creative Developments in Psychotherapy.* New York: Jason Aronson (1973), pp. 439–89. Originally published in P Worchel and D Byrne (eds) *Personality Change.* New York: Wiley (1964).

Gendlin, ET (1968) The experiential response. In EF Hammer (ed) *Use of Interpretation in Treatment: Technique and Art.* New York: Grune & Stratton.

Gendlin, ET (1970) The use of imagery in experiential focusing. *Psychotherapy: Theory, Research and Practice, 7*, 4, 221–3.

Gendlin, ET (1973) A phenomenology of emotions: anger. In D Carr & ES Casey (eds) *Explorations in Phenomenology. Papers for the Society for Phenomenology and Existential Philosophy*. The Hague: Martinus Nijoff, pp. 367–98.

Gendlin, ET (1978/2003) *Focusing*. Revised and updated 25th anniversary edition (2003). London: Rider.

Gendlin, ET (1990) The small steps of the therapy process: How they come and how to help them come. In G Lietaer, J Rombauts & R Van Balen (eds) *Client-Centered and Experiential Psychotherapy in the Nineties*. Leuven: Leuven University Press, pp. 205–224.

Gendlin, ET (1991) Thinking beyond patterns. In B den Ouden and M Moen *The Presence of Feeling in Thought*. New York: Peter Lang, pp. 21–151. Also available as a monograph from the Focusing Institute, New York.

Gendlin, ET (1996) *Focusing-Oriented Psychotherapy*. New York: Guilford Press.

Gendlin, ET (1997) *A Process Model*. New York: Focusing Institute.

Gendlin, ET (2001) The tacit/implicit actually employed in a new kind of thinking. Keynote address at Polanyi Conference, Loyola University, Chicago, 8 June 2001.

Gendlin, ET, Beebe, J III, Cassens, S, Klein, M & Oberlandes, M (1968) Focusing ability in psychotherapy, personality and creativity. *Research in Psychotherapy*, *3*, 217–41

Gendlin, ET & Tomlinson, TM (1967) The process conception and its measurement. In CR Rogers (ed) *The Therapeutic Relationship and its Impact: A study of psychotherapy with schizophrenics*. Madison: University of Wisconsin Press, pp. 109–31.

Goldman, R (2002) The empty-chair dialogue for unfinished business. In JC Watson, RN Goldman & MS Warner (eds) *Client-Centered and Experiential Psychotherapy in the 21st Century*. Ross-on-Wye: PCCS Books.

Greenberg, LS, Rice, LN & Elliott, R (1993) *Facilitating Emotional Change: The moment-by-moment process*. New York: Guilford Press.

Hamlyn, DW (1967) The logical and psychological aspects of learning. In RS Peters (ed) *The Concept of Education*. London: Routledge & Kegan Paul, pp. 24–43.

Hendricks, M (2002) Focusing-oriented/experiential psychotherapy. In DJ Cain & J Seeman (eds) *Humanistic Psychotherapies: Handbook of research and practice*. Washington, DC: American Psychological Association, pp. 221–51.

Hendricks, M (2003) Dialogue between Mary Hendricks Gendlin and Marge Witty. *Person-Centred Practice*, *11*, 2, 61–9.

Iberg, J (2002) Psychometric development of measures of in-session focusing activity: The *Focusing-Oriented Session Report* and the *Therapist Ratings of Client Focusing Activity.* In JC Watson, RN Goldman & M Warner (eds) *Client-Centered and Experiential Psychotherapy in the 21st Century.* Ross-on-Wye: PCCS Books, pp. 221–47.

Joas, H (1985) *GH Mead: A contemporary re-examination of his thought.* Cambridge: Polity Press.

Kant, I (1781/1933) *A Critique of Pure Reason.* Translated (1933) by Norman Kemp Smith. London: Macmillan.

Kirtner, WL & Cartwright, DS (1958) Success and failure in client-centered therapy as a function of initial in-therapy behavior. *Journal of Consulting Psychology, 22,* 329–33.

Klagsbrun, J (n.d.) *How to Teach a Focusing Workshop.* New York: Focusing Institute.

Klein, MH, Mathieu, PL, Gendlin, ET & Kiesler, DJ (1969) *The Experiencing Scale: A research and training manual.* Madison: Wisconsin Pscychiatric Institute.

Klein, MH, Mathieu-Coughlan, P & Kiesler, DJ (1986) The experiencing scales. In LS Greenberg & WM Pinsof (eds) *The Psychotherapeutic Process: A research handbook.* New York: Guilford, pp. 21–71.

Kuhn, TS (1962/1996) *The Structure of Scientific Revolutions* (3rd edn). (1996) Chicago: University of Chicago Press.

Lang, H (1998) *The Order of Nature in Aristotle's Physics.* Cambridge: Cambridge University Press.

Levine, P (1997) *Waking the Tiger: Healing Trauma.* Berkeley, CA: North Atlantic.

Lietaer, G (1998) From non-directive to experiential: a paradigm unfolding. In B Thorne & E Lambers *Person-Centred Therapy: A European Perspective.* London: Sage.

Mathieu-Coughlan, P & Klein, MH (1984) Experiential psychotherapy: Key events in client–therapist interaction. In LN Rice & LS Greenberg (eds) *Patterns of Change.* New York: Guilford, pp. 213–48.

Mead, GH (1934) *Mind, Self and Society.* Chicago IL: University of Chicago Press.

Mearns, D (1994) *Developing Person-Centred Counselling.* London: Sage.

Mearns, D & Thorne, B (1988/2007) *Person-Centred Therapy in Action* (3rd edn) (2007). London: Sage.

Mearns, D & Thorne, B (2000) *Person-Centred Therapy Today.* London: Sage.

Merry, T (2004) Classical client-centred therapy. In P Sanders (ed) *The Tribes of the Person-Centred Nation.* Ross-on-Wye: PCCS Books, pp. 21–44.

Mountford, CP (2006) Dr Rogers and the Rebellious Right Arm. *Self and Society, 34* (2), Sept–Oct 2006.

Murphy, FH (2006) Healing and Growing in Nature: A personal exploration of the process of symbolisation at the edge of awareness. MA dissertation,

School of Education and Lifelong Learning, University of East Anglia.

Orlinsky, D, Grawe, K & Parks, BK (1994) Process and outcome in psychotherapy—noch einmal. In AE Bergin & SL Garfield *Handbook of Psychotherapy and Behavior Change.* (4th edn). Chichester: John Wiley, pp. 270–376.

Polanyi, M (1958) *Personal Knowledge.* London: Routledge & Kegan Paul.

Polanyi, M (1967) *The Tacit Dimension.* London: Routledge & Kegan Paul.

Popper, KR (1959) *The Logic of Scientific Discovery.* London: Hutchinson.

Purton, C (2000) Empathising with shame and guilt. In J Marquez-Teixeira & S Antunes (eds). *Client-Centered and Experiential Psychotherapy.* Linda a Velha: Vale & Vale, pp. 33–54.

Purton, C (2004) *Person-Centred Therapy: The Focusing-Oriented Approach.* Basingstoke: Palgrave Macmillan.

Rogers, CR (1956) The essence of psychotherapy: Moments of movement. Paper given at the first meeting of the American Academy of Psychotherapists, New York, October 20, 1956.

Rogers, CR (1957) The necessary and sufficient conditions of therapeutic personality change. *Journal of Consulting Psychology, 21,* 95–103.

Rogers, CR (1958) A process conception of psychotherapy. *American Psychologist, 18,* 142–59.

Rogers, CR (1959) A theory of therapy, personality and interpersonal relationships, as developed in the client-centered framework. In S Koch (ed) *Psychology: A study of a science, Vol. 3. Formulations of the person and the social context.* New York: McGraw-Hill, pp. 184–256.

Rogers, CR (1961) *On Becoming a Person.* London: Constable.

Rogers, CR (1968) Michael Polanyi and Carl Rogers: A dialogue. In W R Coulson & CR Rogers (eds) *Man and the Science of Man.* Columbus, Ohio: Charles E. Merrill Publishing Co, pp. 193–201.

Rogers, CR (1986a) Reflection of feelings. *Person-Centered Review, 1,* 4, 375–7.

Rogers, CR (1986b) Client-centered therapy. In IL Kutash & A Wolf *Psychotherapist's Casebook.* San Francisco: Jossey-Bass, pp. 197–208.

Rothschild, B (2000) *The Body Remembers: The psychophysiology of trauma and trauma treatment.* New York: WW Norton.

Sachse, R (1990a) Concrete interventions are crucial: The influence of the therapist's processing proposals on the client's intrapersonal exploration in client-centered therapy. In G Lietaer, J Rombauts & R Van Balen, *Client-Centred and Experiential Psychotherapy in the Nineties.* Leuven: Leuven University Press, pp. 295–308.

Sachse, R (1990b) The influence of therapist processing proposals on the explication process of the client. *Person-Centered Review 5,* 3, 321–44.

Sanders, P (ed) (2004) *The Tribes of the Person-Centred Nation.* Ross-on-Wye: PCCS Books.

Sanders, P (2006) *The Person-Centred Counselling Primer.* Ross-on-Wye:

PCCS Books.

Stinckens, N, Lietaer, G & Leijssen, M (2002) Working with the inner critic: Fighting the enemy or keeping it company. In JC Watson, RN Goldman & M Warner (eds) *Client-Centered and Experiential Psychotherapy in the 21st Century: Advances in theory, research and practice.* Ross-on-Wye: PCCS Books, pp. 415–26.

Warner, MS (2000) Person-centered psychotherapy: One nation, many tribes. *Person-Centered Journal 7*, 1, 28–39.

Worsley, R (2004) Integrating with integrity. In P Sanders (ed) *The Tribes of the Person-Centred Nation.* Ross-on-Wye: PCCS Books, pp. 125–47.

INDEX